BEAUTY, WONDER AND BELONGING

A Book of Hours for the Monastery of the Cosmos

Beauty, Wonder and Belonging

A Book of Hours for the Monastery of the Cosmos

by James Conlon

The Rhodes-Fulbright Library

Cover Design by Billie Sommerfeld

Cover Image by NASA

.

ISBN: 978-155605-395-5

Library of Congress Control Number:2009928964

WYNDHAM HALL PRESS
Lima, Ohio 45806
www.wyndhamhallpress.com

Printed in The United States of America

BEAUTY, WONDER AND BELONGING

A Book of Hours for the Monastery of the Cosmos

by James Conlon

Books by James Conlon

Geo-Justice: A Preferential Option for the Earth

Earth Story, Sacred Story

Lyrics for Re-Creation:
Language for the Music of the Universe

Ponderings from the Precipice:
Soulwork for a New Millennium

Sacred Impulse:
A Planetary Spirituality of Heart and Fire

At the Edge of Our Longing:
Unspoken Hunger for Sacredness and Depth

From the Stars to the Streets:
Engaged Wisdom for a Brokenhearted World

Beauty, Wonder and Belonging:
A Book of Hours for the Monastery of the Cosmos

ACKNOWLEGEMENTS

I am grateful to all whom I have been privileged to name as companions in the preparation of this book, in particular Kitty Nagler, Valerie Bowman, John Bowman, Joan LaFlamme, Marilyn Goddard, Jane Heckathorn, Kathryn Letkey, Billie Sommerfeld, Christine Steady Ndiage, Mark McCullough and his colleagues at Wyndham Hall Press.

Table of Contents

Foreword

Throughout the ages the entire planetary community, both human and "otherkind," has responded to the mystical moments of dawn and dusk when the numinous dimension of the Universe opens and reveals itself with special intimacy.

We can feel the great shifts at these two hinge moments of the day, as the veil within the sanctuary of the cosmic temple lifts, and a heightened sense of Presence is experienced within the Earth community.

Beauty, Wonder and Belonging invites the reader to step over the threshold of these two sacred moments of dawn and dusk and join with the entire planetary community in the celebration of Being. In reading *Beauty, Wonder and Belonging* there is a rhythmic sense of expansion and contraction, activism and reflection, and a heightened awareness that we live within these great circular gestures of Earth's dynamics.

Beauty, Wonder and Belonging is a cosmic psalter for those living and working in the monastery that is Earth herself. It draws upon the brilliance and gift of the monastic traditions of the planet that for ages have organized the day around the rhythms of Earth's turning. These traditions have given voice to the human experience in an ongoing chorus of praise and celebration through the Liturgy of the Hours.

Beauty, Wonder and Belonging invites us to become aware of ourselves as the very dimensions of the planet of which we are a part. We, who are integral with Earth and ourselves, are that "Book of Hours." When our own rhythms and flow are in sync with Earth's hours, then a natural activism arises that is sane, steady and balanced. Our work in the world is energized and fueled by the depth we cultivate at the hinge moments of dawn and dusk. In keeping with this rhythm our activism becomes trustworthy. There is no burn out or exaggeration of ourselves as the ones doing the work.

Beauty, Wonder and Belonging celebrates life within Earth's 4.5-billion year fidelity to its cyclical rotation. Within this faithful turning of the planet, dawn and dusk, seasons and cycles have made their debut with accuracy and precision.

Yet, within the larger dynamics of the cosmos, another rhythm that is not cyclical but developmental has been simultaneously unfolding, and it is this dynamic that we also need to celebrate. While the steady pulse of dawn and dusk has kept beat over the ages, other wild rhythms have emerged under this steady beat.

Hold the pulse of dawn and dusk and hear beneath it the birth of the oceans, the emergence of single cells, the first molecule capturing sunlight, the creation of a backbone, the first feet to walk on land, the coming of the flowers, dinosaurs roaming, the emergence of the human, the discovery of fire, the sprouting of seeds.

Beauty, Wonder and Belonging unfolds within these larger dynamics of cosmogenesis where time is not contained within a twenty-four hour cycle but set free without constraints.

To this end, *Beauty, Wonder and Belonging* is itself a book at the threshold. It lies between the steady cycles of Earth's turning and the wild unfolding dynamics of the Universe moving toward its numinous destiny.

—Gail Worcelo

Closing: Dawn and Dusk
~Mystical moments of dawn and dusk are when the Universe reveals itself.
~Each moment is an opportunity to step over the threshold to a place where the Great Work is organized and fulfilled.
~The more expansive context for our journey is the developmental dynamic that marks and celebrates sunlight, the coming of the flowers, the emergence of the human, discovery of fire and the sprouting of seeds as our cosmic book of hours marks the unfolding dynamics of the Universe moving toward its destiny.

Dedication to Thomas Berry

Where is Thomas?

Thomas, Where are you now?
A child raising himself
Walking through the meadow

Thomas, Where are you now?
Reading at 2:30am
with a towel at the door
Or seated in the diner with a companion
and a good glass of wine

Thomas, Where are you now?
brooding over Earth
the Jeremiah of our time
asking the question
"what should I say?"

Thomas, Where are you now?
in the Philippines or China
Riverdale or the Caroline hills
where your dreams and thoughts were born

Thomas, Where are you now?
in your fierce and wild life
you are here among us
your spirit clear and strong
calling us to our Great Work
from the Cathedral of the Soul

Thomas Berry is generally understood to be the most significant scholar and spokesperson for the movement that sees the future of humanity and the entire planetary community as unfolding from a new, shared cosmic story. We are deeply indebted for his lifetime of dedication that makes possible a more mutually enhancing relationship between humanity and the other-than-human world.

Thomas' life has been devoted to being a passionate herald for Earth, reminding us of the beauty of the cosmos, the enchantment of the Universe, and the challenges, dangers and possibilities that await the children and all those yet to be born of every species. Thomas is a voice for the voiceless, a spokesperson for the deep wisdom that resides in women, indigenous people, our Christian roots, other religious traditions and the new science. He emboldens us to nourish our souls and amplify our spirits within the mystery and beauty of each meadow, sunset and star.

Calling forth a renewed awareness of our destiny and the legacy that is our rightful inheritance, Thomas warns us of the danger of "soul death" during this era of human pathos and ecological bereavement. If we devastate the planet, we endanger and extinguish our souls. When we diminish our sensitivity, imagination and inner depth, we lessen our capacity to fully experience Earth. Thomas challenges each of us to take back our souls and, in doing so, the soul of our planet.

Out of the chaos of this present moment comes an enormous opportunity for creativity that could foster harmony and integration for the entire Earth community. We are being offered a "moment of grace," a time of both creativity and promise. Thomas reminds us that we have been chosen to live at this particular moment, each endowed with a unique and significant role to play in what he calls the Great Work. We are given the opportunity to contribute to the difficult transition from the post-industrial era to the ecological age that awaits us. The new era offers nourishment and sustainability, engaging our human capacity for play, delight and good work. Thomas promises that if we undertake this Great Work, we will know where we are, where we have been, and where we are going. "We begin to understand that the way to the world of the sacred is through the place of our dwelling. We are finally awakening to the beauty of the land."

During a recent visit with Thomas, once again he emphases his hope that humans focus our full attention on Earth and her people. It is critical that we, particularly in the Western world, take our proper place in the sacred Universe, realizing that the "American dream" will no longer work. At this defining moment we must heed the call to be liberated from convenient cultural structures that stand in the way of change. Thomas encourages us to evoke, name and celebrate a new way of being present, urged on by belief in a God we do not know. And as our systems of knowledge change, Thomas states, so must our spirituality. Through the expression of poetry, music, movement and art, we connect to other modes of understanding; we gain access to the wonder and beauty of Earth and all her peoples. Thomas joyously exclaimed: "May we all give thanks for our gorgeous planet and along the way to our Earth companions."

Gratitude and Goodness
Frail and tender one
man of Wonder and Dream
as you ponder the meaning
of your journey and
the way you wish to be remembered
I join a chorus of gratitude and thanks
with your passion for Earth
you leave us a legacy of love
faith in the uncreated one
your vision strong and true
spreads beauty and goodness
all around

Jim,

Thomas and I today once again delved deeply into your Beauty, Wonder and Belonging and savored with fresh appreciation the power and poetry of this unique tribute to creation, immersed as it is in monastic Church history as well as in the new story of evolution.

Thank you for this gift and know that it lies within easy reach on Thomas's bookcase, and is and will be often picked up to enhance the hours of our days.

Gratefully,
Margaret (Berry)

Introduction

"We have forgotten the great spiritual impact of these moments of transition. The dawn is mystical, a very special moment for the human to experience the wonder and depth of fulfillment in the sacred. The same is true of nightfall... We deny ourselves our deepest delight by not participating in the dawn, the dusk, the solstice, the spring time."
(Thomas Berry)

We live in a time of a heightened religious sensitivity when many people are awakening to the sacred, embracing an authentic spirituality. Simultaneously we live in a time when global warming threatens to tip the fragile balance of Earth. Poverty, hunger and disease prevail around the planet; political, financial and local systems are collapsing on a global scale; war, genocide and vast population migrations flood the daily news media; crime and human-created personal hardship rip apart the neighborhoods of our home communities; species are becoming extinct at an alarming decline not seen for tens of millions of years.

Still, in the face of these global erosions of the sacred, a spiritual renaissance is arising in our midst. In small gatherings and movements around the world, something anew and exciting is taking place. In his groundbreaking book, Paul Hawken calls it the "blessed unrest"; Joanna Macy and David Korten name this new moment as the "great turning". The Institute of Noetic Science calls this new consciousness, "the shift". Thomas Berry, geologian and cultural historian, names this "moment of grace" as the emergence of the "ecozoic era," a time to create a mutually enhancing world. Whatever name we give this transformation of culture and consciousness, we can say with certitude that it continues to have a subtle yet profound impact on the prayer life of the people.

The new science, a prophetic partner in this new movement, is accumulating a growing knowledge of evolution and quantum physics. As the origin story of our Universe, galaxies, Earth, life, human species unfolds daily through the discoveries made by science, we realize that all creation is held within an inclusive relationship. This story celebrates all life, energy and matter as a sacred wisdom that is fresh and palpable. This revelatory narrative tells of God's creation - how we came into being, where we are now - and provides a glimpse of the future. Our new story transcends all separation and division, opening us up to a unifying vision of hope, truth and wisdom. Yet, we are aware that when our mode of knowing changes, so must our spiritual practice.

Ancient prayer practices often involved contemplation and silence. We find this mode of prayer in the "desert fathers" and the ancient monastic traditions. Each medieval monastery celebrated the book of hours at specific times of the day. The book of hours allowed for prayerful pauses at specific sacred moments. It saw the dawn and dusk of each day not only as a reminder of the cycle of time but also as a moment of deep awareness of the Divine.

Many long today to revitalize their prayer life. They feel called to a contemplative practice with a "monastic flavor." Their call is not so much to enter a monastic community but rather to engage in a spiritual practice that views the Universe and all creation as a context of prayer, a monastery of the cosmos.

This book was prompted by a deep and growing conviction that the experience of beauty, wonder and belonging is an important component of our spirituality. I offer this book as a companion for the journey. It is not so much to be read as pondered. You are invited to pray always, not so much prayers of rote or recitation, but rather a prayer of conscious awareness, of mystery and a deep felt sense, of pathos and beauty, of wonder and engagement, of fragmentation and belonging.

Beauty, Wonder and Belonging focuses on the mystical moments revealed to us when two worlds meet at the dawn and dusk of each day – for it is between these sacred moments of dawn and dusk that our lives of engagement are lived out. These pages provide a guide for those who strive to connect the emerging cosmological vision with their personal practice. The twice-daily pause for prayer creates a rhythm that opens a portal to wild imagination, a doorway to the Divine. With silence, our senses open to the ever present now; we approach our lives with the curiosity of a child, the heart of a mystic and the voice of a prophet. This book invites you into a monastery of the cosmos without walls.

In therapy, we retrace our steps, we return to the beginning and then move forward. As people of the new story, we are required to walk a similar path. It is by returning that we can be delivered to ourselves with renewed energy to discover our destiny and become increasingly clear about out lives. We explore not only the origins of our own life but also the originating energy of the Universe. When we move backward in time from the origin of the human to earlier life formations to Earth to the original flaring forth, our search takes us into an encounter with mystery — this mystery can be understood as the originating energy of the Universe. This experience of mystery can be understood as the Divine.

Today I wonder whether there might be a Rosa Parks among us who came from nowhere to inspire and initiate a civil rights movement or a Rachel Carson who became the founder of the modern environmental movement. Perhaps it is the simple joy and wonder of a child watching a duck land on a pond that will activate the deep wells of wisdom.

> This morning in the sky, as the earth turns eastward, so instinctive the manner whereby humans and all living creatures face the glory of transforming dawn and in the evening bow to the mysteries of night.

With these words Thomas Berry challenges us to fall into the rhythm of the Universe. As you reflect on his words and the pages that follow, spend some time on this question: What does it mean to be a cosmological person? Allow your imagination to be free to ponder what you are called to be at this defining moment in human-Earth history.

How to Use This Book

The book of hours you hold in your hands is aligned with the patterns revealed in and through the heart of the Universe itself. Each day reflects a particular theme.

- **Sunday – The Universe Story:** The Universe flares forth from the original fireball of heat and light; everything erupts, emerges and unfolds into ultimate mystery.
- **Monday – Mystery:** Out of mystery Earth awakens in bursts of fire and creativity.
- **Tuesday – The Sacred:** From chaos and creativity sacredness emerges and life is born on Earth.
- **Wednesday – The Human:** Through conscious self-awareness of the human, planet Earth becomes conscious of herself.

- **Thursday – This Moment:** At this defining moment humanity gives shape and form to the shared story of our Earth community.
- **Friday – Struggle and Fulfillment:** Through struggle and fulfillment we create a new chapter in our sacred, seamless and evolutionary life.
- **Saturday – Cultural Therapy:** We discover and celebrate a world view that provides a new context for healing in our time.

This book of hours uses certain terms as components of dawn and dusk for each day that form the structure of the book.

- ***Theme: The Voice of the Universe*** announces the focus of the day.
- ***Reflection: Canticle to Creation*** provides images and symbols for the theme of each day.
- ***Threshold Thoughts:*** "If you would be a poet, discover a new way for mortals to inhabit the earth." Lawerence Ferlinghetti.
- ***Story: Revelatory Moments of the Universe*** recalls the past, envisions the future and locates our lives within the present moment.
- ***Prophetic Voices: In Tune with the Cosmos*** presents insights from mystics and prophets that deepen our understanding of the theme of the day.
- ***A Moment of Silence:*** "I'm listening but I don't know if what I hear is silence or God." William Stafford
- ***Response: Toward a Mutually Enhancing World*** moves us into action to become a healing presence engaged in this Great Work.

As you journey through the dawn and dusk of each day, you will discover how to awaken to the rising sun and all the infinite possibilities. In the evening, as darkness descends upon Earth, you peer into the darkness of which Rilke writes, "I have faith in nights."

May you venture with joy and open-heartedness on this journey.

Closing Thoughts:
~As we experience ***Beauty, Wonder and Belonging,*** *the Universe becomes a monastery without walls, an unexpected epicenter of hope, engagement, sacredness and depth.*
~Today we are invited to approach our lives with the curiosity of a child, the heart of a mystic and the voice of a prophet.
~Every star, child or creek becomes a page from scripture, a paragraph of wisdom; each encounter is enacted in the theater of the soul.
~Thomas Berry writes, "The difficulty is that the natural world is seen primarily for human use, not as mode of sacred presence primarily to be communed with in wonder and beauty and intimacy…a sacred reality to be venerated."

And so we begin…

SUNDAY

DAWN

Theme: The Universe Story

"In the beginning there was the Word. The Word was in God's presence and the Word was God . . . through the Word all things came into being."
(Gospel of John)

Our human story is the Universe Story that begins 13.7 billion years ago. As we discover this story, we discover our origin and evolution in time and are able to view our lives within this cosmic narrative. Energized by a sense of the Divine, we are moved to celebrate and experience the emergent source of ultimate mystery. We locate our lives within the dynamics of the unfolding Universe and gain a glimpse of the future coupled with a deep gratitude for our ancestors. With this in mind we move slowly forward into the future with renewed confidence and trust.

Reflection: The Universe Story

The Universe Story is our sacred story. It began with a great flash of light that filled the Universe. From the extreme heat, helium and hydrogen were born. Galaxies and stars emerged. Earth came into existence and gave birth to oceans, forests and a profusion of living species. The human species marked a new era of the great unfolding story. Today we are challenged to participate in the Earth community.

The Universe Story comes to us not in words but rather in the language of the cosmos. The cosmos speaks a colorful language of image and sound, touch and taste, fragrance and movement, daily and seasonal rhythms together with the deep wisdom obtained through the unfolding dynamics of the Universe and insights into the mystery that lies at the heart of matter.

Each of us has experienced the sacred nature of the Universe. As we learn more through the wisdom of the ancients and the new science, the story reveals a new vision of reality, one that can heal our alienation and replace this uneasy illusion of separation with a sense of community. We create a vessel of radical inclusiveness for all life and open ourselves to the Divine presence that manifests itself in all things and in all species.

Intuitively we become aware that the Universe Story weaves bands of meaning, identity and purpose into a seamless tapestry, unveiling a lavish garment of infinite possibilities that can only be contained within an evolutionary universe. This unfolding creation story provides a context in which to celebrate joy, consecrate sorrow and discover our place and destiny.

The Universe Story is a portal to a new era and a new culture. Within this story we each have an unique role to play in the Great Work. We become participants when first we identify and assess the most important issue of our time, namely the ecological crisis with its interconnected issues of poverty, disease, gender inequality, and the inequities of culture, class and privilege. We then dedicate the meaning and purpose of our lives to heal and eradicate these debilitating global calamities.

As we experience the Universe, our hearts and minds become infused with its powers. Aware, as Thomas Berry writes, that we "are shaped and formed in the same primordial furnace," we envision a world where beauty shines forth and the future is better than all the pasts. From this place of all possibilities, we become a unified people in the Great Work to create a better world.

Threshold Thoughts

Letter at "The Well"
God of the Cosmos
speak to me
tell me tales of hope and salvation

Do not blind my eyes
to the pain of the planet
nor plunge me into a
withering and unraveling life

God of the Cosmos
tell me about the questions
I have not dared to ask

Tell me who I am
And why I am here

Tell me of the cosmos
and the soul

Tell me about tomorrow
as I embrace today

Tell me a story
that I can savor
celebrate and understand

God of the Cosmos
bring me home
to the Universe and myself

Open the ear of my heart
to the Masters
of the cosmos and the soul

God of the Cosmos
make me one
teach me

Story: The Night Sky and the Flashlight

One evening a young boy was outside in the backyard with his father. He was holding a flashlight so that his father could see to make some repairs on the family car. Momentarily, he looked up into the night sky and encountered the endless depth of the ultimate mystery. Enthralled in the vast wonder and beauty before him, the young boy dropped the flashlight.

That boy intuited that the Universe is indeed a source of sacredness and depth, a container of power and beauty that empowers and energizes life. That moment shaped this boy's journey and, even today, he remains enveloped in the rapture of that moment.

Prophetic Voices

The rocks themselves are a primary expression of spirit. To have a spiritual experience we have to have spiritual depth. Awaken to the ordinary and be stunned. (Brian Swimme)

God's nothingness fills the entire world; his something, though, is nowhere. (Meister Eckhart)

The scientific story of creation is magnificent and enormous and provides a context for all religions to articulate their experience of the sacred. (Richard Harmon)

The Body of Christ is ultimately the entire universe . . . St. Paul tells us that in Christ "all things hold together." The sacred community ultimately is the entire universe. (Thomas Berry)

The new scientific cosmology shows us a universe in which we have an origin, an inclusive home and meaningful destiny. (Paul Brockelman)

The beauty of the world is the first witness of blessing. (John O'Donohue)

A Moment of Silence

Response: Making Sense of Mystery

Energy is the template of existence. Our lives, creativity and the quality of each moment are a function of the flow of energy in our lives. Burnout, fatigue and free-floating depression are the result of energy that is blocked or stuck. Exercise, diet and spiritual practice are ways to keep our energy flowing. Vitality, enthusiasm and being alive to each moment result from the constant movement of energy and the healing of unrest and irritation.

Thomas Berry offers guidance to our spiritual practice, telling us in *Befriending the Earth* something about how he prays:

> The sense of the divine is a sense of mystery…The divine comes to us through the universe manifestation. We are surrounded, immersed in the divine from the beginning of our existence. I pray by a simple awareness of the deep mystery of things, the absorption and wonder of the universe for the mind, the beauty for the imagination and intimacy for the emotions.

What is blocking your energy and interfering with your joy of life? Name it, ponder the effect of it on your body and life systems and consider those changes needed to heal yourself. How can your spiritual practice support your healthy flow of life? Reflect and pray on these questions.

DUSK

Theme: The Universe Story

"We are here to hear the Story and experience the dream." (Thomas Berry)

Story is the most human act of communion in which we engage. As the existing origin stories and myths hold less relevance for us, we search for a great master narrative to re-invigorate us — one that is inclusive, that embraces all our stories. Alla Rene Bozarth simply expresses it: "The stories you tell one another around fires in the dark will make you strong and wise."

Reflection: The New Context

In the current environment there is a deep yearning, a profound desire to liberate the planet and the forces that hold her captive and oppressed. We are aware that if the systems of knowledge change, we must express ourselves differently in this new context. What is needed at this time is a joyfully experienced cosmological context—a new and energetic perspective on life that will make all things possible and new.

Thus begins a new epoch — a renewed time when Earth will be viewed as a great cosmic unfolding, a time when she will be once again enveloped in an ocean of mystery, a sea of unlimited possibility.

Today, humanity is increasingly aware of the challenges and crises that confront our planet. We stand alert, awake to the emerging sources of mysterious energies being revealed in the new science. These unfolding revelations empower our capacity to transform and transcend, opening us to the unprecedented opportunities ahead.

Threshold Thoughts

What Should I Say
Words escape my grasp
I ask the blossom
what should I say?
the answer comes back
tell the story.

I ask the lemon tree
standing stately in the garden
what should I say?
tree answers
tell the story.

Listen deeply now
beauty shines forth
from every molecule of creation
shouting a chorus of wonder.

Again I gaze and ask
what should I say?

The answer comes back
now dimly heard
remember little one
you and all creation
together tell the story
listen deeply with your heart.

Story: And Thus We Learn

My father loved stories. In his later years Dad would invite neighbors to join him on the front porch to share their stories. As a child I too loved stories—stories told around a campfire, stories told by farmers as they looked over their land on Sunday morning. As I grew older, I began to understand that my family had a story. So did our village and country. I also realized that Sunday morning was about storytelling. After all, wasn't Jesus a storyteller! In fact, the Gospels are really books of stories.

Stories are the primary way we learn. They shape the contours of our consciousness and alter the landscape of our souls. Stories refresh and satisfy. They are instruments of grief, joy, healing, hope. Stories reveal who we are and what we are called to be; they express what lies deep within.

As a community organizer, I realized that within the story of a community and its people lies a primary resource for justice and change. More recently, the new science and new cosmology have taught me that the Universe has a spiritual story too—one that reveals and connects us to the Divine. Earth herself is a sacred story. In her story the human race is seen emerging from the physical and psychic dimensions of the earth. Within that story are the seeds for personal and communal healing.

An urgent challenge for our time is to integrate the Universe Story with what I call the story of geo-justice. Geo-justice is born when the dynamics of the Universe — interconnectiveness, diversity and depth— are supported and expressed to allow every member of the Earth community to fulfill its destiny and purpose. It is that moment when beauty shines forth.

Prophetic Voices

We explain things by telling their story—how they come into being and the changes that have taken place over time—whether minute or millennia—this is especially true in explaining those profound formative influences that have shaped our sense of the sacred. (Thomas Berry)

When we begin to tell our stories our imagination begins to flow out to our eyes and ears to inhabit the breathing earth once again. (David Abram)

The universe is made up of stories, not atoms. (Muriel Rukeyser)

The sea has not lost its capacity to amaze. (Philip Marsden)

A Moment of Silence

Response: Telling Our Stories

Storytelling is the most radical and accessible approach available to organize our memories, the events of our day, dreams of possibilities and hope for what can be. By telling our stories and reflecting imaginatively on our lives, our ancestral roots and our relationship to the land, we discover elements that have previously gone unnoticed. We may discover powerful memories of nurture in our childhood or of selflessness in parenthood. I remember a student telling her story, and in the telling, she re-discovered her grandmother's commitment to justice in a textile union. By listening to one another's' stories and by telling our own stories, we uncover approaches that can motivate and energize our actions.

I urge you to take this opportunity to write your own story, both for yourself and for the individuals and groups with whom you live, work and play. What is your personal story? How has beauty shown itself in your life? Reflect on your unique role in the Great Work and the difference that your life has played.

Closing of the Day ~The Universe Speaks the Great Story

~ We begin with Sunday, the Sacred Story and we locate our day, our work, our life within the dynamics of the great cosmic adventure.

~ We view our lives within the great cosmic narrative and we discover our origins, our unfolding in time, thus gaining a glimpse of the future.

~ We enter this cosmic context where we celebrate joy, consecrate sorrow, discover who we are and find our place in the Great Work to create a more mutually enhancing world for all Earth species.

~ We reflect on the realization that "we were shaped and formed in the same primordial furnace." We have more in common with each other than not.

~ Our new story is told when we re-experience the rapture of the night sky or a conversation on the front porch of our home and through the stories we tell each other around a campfire or the family hearth or over the lunch table.

MONDAY

DAWN

Theme: Mystery

"What we utter is God's wisdom, a mysterious hidden wisdom." (Letter to the Corinthians)

Mystery is what is not experienced in itself but is manifest in everything else. It is where the sacred is revealed. Beauty is the unique manifestation of Divine mystery; it shines through each expression of creation. Belonging happens when creation reveals Divine mystery through its infinite interconnections.

Mystery remains elusive and knows not boundaries nor can it be captured through concrete naming. Yet, like the ocean or the night sky, mystery consistently invites us into a deeper and deeper immersion. We know in our soul that central to the spiritual journey is the deep awareness that our lives are enveloped in mystery. As John O'Donohue wrote, "Each day is a path of wonder."

Reflection: Solstice Moments

When we recall the experience of our childhood, that special time of transparent openness, spontaneity and fresh energy, both wild and free, we come to a place of encounter with the Divine. This poignant memory is a connection with the God who is beyond all things yet simultaneously available and present in all that we are and all that we do. This is as close to a tangible encounter with mystery as we can firmly grasp.

Life is about mystery. Caught up in the continuous process of life, we often wonder about the meaning of events like birth, aging, death and what happens beyond the grave; the given answers are nebulous, confusing and rarely satisfying. Other life circumstances that show up, most often unexpectedly, are illness and disease, personal loss, natural disasters, ecological events, and fractures in the psyche caused by early trauma, unexpected heartbreak as well as tragedy brought about by the disintegration of relationships, physical health, economic or social status. Yet assuredly, also contained within the folds of mystery, are the opaqueness of love, the joy of falling in love and the deep promptings of the heart that lead us forward to our calling, destiny and relationships.

Each time, when confronted with these unexpected and often inexplicable experiences, we meet the face of mystery. Although it is helpful to draw on the wisdom of the past and the insights gained through contemporary science, they do not provide an answer — they simply summon us to the threshold of the Divine.

At this stage of my life, a period of unprecedented change, my question has shifted to, what is the human response to mystery? Sages offer us counsel. For some, it is prayer, silence, meditation, living into the question. For others, it is an open posture to a listening heart, a sacred presence, a shadow of uncertainty, a sunrise of hope. For all, it is prayer to the unknown God who evokes the mystery of life. No matter how we position ourselves within this place of uncertainty, our response can only be understood as courage in the face of the unknown.

Threshold Thoughts

A Declaration
There's a glimmer in the window
Earth wakes up
greets the day

Everywhere new light
washes across creation

Squirrel shouts "Good morning"
love proclaims the angelus
a new day is born
each creature
a member of the choir
proclaiming songs of praise

Resurrection
Birds sing
breezes blow
sun announces the day
beauty envelops the meadow
new life springs forth with a symphony of Easter
the sweat lodge door lies open to recall the empty tomb
and resurrection rises once again

Story: Prayer

Prayer once puzzled me, particularly the prayer of petition. Is prayer a way to change God's mind? I wondered. I prayed for my mother when she had cancer, but she didn't get well. Was my prayer answered? Did God say no? My catechism said that prayer was "the elevation of the heart and mind to God." What did that mean?

Later I began to understand that prayer was more about gratitude and praise than about "give me and forgive me." It was not about changing God's mind but rather about changing how I engaged in the process of life.

Today I believe that prayer is largely about conscious self-awareness, about paying attention to the Divine that is already present. In fact, prayer is more about listening and responding than words. It opens us to the epiphany moments in every aspect of our lives and throughout all creation. Prayer allows us to awaken to who we are and live more fully into our story each day. Prayer infuses us with the energy needed to live with depth, hope, inspiration and purpose.

Prayer is an opportunity to acknowledge our membership in the community of creation, to live reflectively with Earth. It is more about being than doing, more about presence than petition, more about wonder and awe than redemption. Teilhard de Chardin counsels us to spend more time on creation and less on redemption. Prayer is living with spontaneity and compassion. Prayer is engaging with the God of transforming mystery.

Prophetic Voices

The sense of the Divine is a sense of mystery . . .. I pray by a simple awareness of the deep mystery of things, the absorption and wonder of the universe for the mind, the beauty for the imagination and intimacy for the emotion. (Thomas Berry)

The universe is not only more mysterious than we know, but more mysterious than we'll ever know. (Brian Swimme)

The Universe is not a machine. It is mystery. The appropriate response to mystery of any kind is wonder — wonder is a form of consciousness that is without words or images, or understanding. When we recognize God as mystery, our spontaneous response is awe and wonder. (Albert Nolan)

Wonder helps us to become aware that we are the earth teaching ourselves. (Sarah Pirtle)

Our goal should be to live life in radical amazement. (Rabbi Abraham Heschel)

Our not knowing God who is boundless mystery is not a pure negation, not simply an empty absence, but a positive characteristic of a relationship between one subject and another…an unending adventure of exploration for yearning, seeking, weeping, laughing, knowing, loving and hoping human beings. (Elizabeth Johnston)

The world of the poor places us before a mystery, and they themselves express a mystery.
(Jon Sobrino)

A grass-blade's no easier to make than an oak. (James Russell Lowell)

The moment one gives close attention to anything, even a blade of grass, it becomes a mysterious, awesome, indescribably magnificent world in itself. (Henry Miller)

A Moment of Silence

Response: Living into the Mystery

Unexpected and unexplained experiences confront us with the face of mystery. In our quest to understand, we engage in prayer, silence, meditation, living the questions and facing the unknown. While both engaged and silent, we wait with great anticipation for beauty, wonder and belonging to pour forth. Mystery occurs at each embodied moment—each one an encounter with the Divine.

Today, spend a few moments to reflect on your encounter with mystery. Was it when you walked the dog this morning as the sun graced you from the east? Or perhaps it was the laughter of an infant as she reached to touch the birds in the clouds? Did your senses spontaneously open to the trees or the rain or the seashore or the breeze? Perhaps an unexpected turn of events bestowed its presence into your day? What were your unique moments? How have these points in time become an integral dimension of your spiritual practice?

DUSK

Theme: Mystery

"Each of us must take our place in the unfolding mystery that is at the heart of the universe." (Miriam MacGillis)

Wonder excites the soul. From it flows intimacy that envelops us as we experience the intense immediacy held within a meadow flower, an orange-mottled kitten, a steep raw mountain cliff, a dear old companion or the crystal clear night sky. In that instant we tremble in the face of the limitless depth into which we sink and feel summoned.

Beauty shines forth from every manifestation of creation. Our spirit soars and divinity is present. We experience the aliveness of our depths and know again with fresh energy, as if for the first time, the invisible embrace of creation and mystery. "Beauty," Teilhard de Chardin tells us, "will reveal itself eloquently in the forerunner and generation of ideas."

Belonging is the connective tissue that weaves each of us into the tapestry of life. We imagine a continuous circle of celebration in which every creature — plum tree, puppy and parent — becomes cousin and kin. We remember that true mutuality transcends the illusion of separateness. When radical inclusiveness dissolves all boundaries, belonging makes itself known and felt.

Reflection: Monastery of the Cosmos

In classical traditions the monastery is a central context for prayer and spiritual practice. It is a place to respond to the two "hinged moments" of the day — dawn and dusk. The monastery provides sacred pauses to celebrate the existence of these great cosmic gestures expressed daily by Earth herself as well as a quiet moment to become aware of ourselves intertwined with all creation that surrounds us.

The Monastery of the Cosmos is a context to honor the connectedness of all life and become cosmological persons engaged at the edge of mystery. From the cosmic monastery the Divine creative spirit leads each of us as pilgrims in search of a more inclusive wisdom, one that is consistently energized and enriched by the Universe Story.

When we confront the questions of mystery through the Universe Story, we address the Divine and open ourselves to explore our intimate connection with the natural world. Divinity is also evolving and continues to emerge just as we do. The unfolding Divine can be perceived in many ways: passionate force, energy, yearning, the present moment, our higher power, nature within and without, light and much more. When we align our energies within the evolving dynamics of the Universe, we ultimately find what is true for our destiny.

The Universe is guiding us into something mysterious and beautiful—a journey into our deepest primal passion, an ecstatic and personal experience of ultimate destiny, purpose and identity. From the vantage point of the Monastery of the Cosmos, prayer is transformed into gratitude, appreciation and presence.

Threshold Thoughts

Gratitude
Energies of appreciation
undulate across our collective soul
thank you echoes everywhere
as we today declare
life is a gift

friendship weaves a sacred path
even those while leaving
always stay behind
paradox appears
endings become beginnings
departures, arrivals
goodbyes, hellos
suddenly I know all is not lost
suddenly I know
what seems invisible
is present everywhere
we are all of us
enveloped in mystery
alive, awake
and oh, so grateful

Shadows and Sunshine
Shadows and sunshine
permeate my depths
and find expression
in the contours of Earth
every moment life begins
at each instant something dies
and in between
God unites us all

Story: For the Rest of Your Life

It was December and the sky had darkened early when a wise, prophetic voice entered the classroom of Sophia Center. It was Carolyn McDade, a passionate woman of wisdom with the gift to lift the hearts and minds of people with her song. As she stood at the piano and belted out "This Ancient Love" and her many other songs, something profound and moving entered the room. Touched deeply, a class member asked if Carolyn would share something of her life story. Her response was generous and revelatory.

Carolyn shared that her life has been one of placing herself in the midst of social movements where people bravely chose to put themselves on the line. She said that her life has been blessed and she is always grateful for the privilege to be with people who put themselves forward for mighty causes and who are accountable for their actions. Her life has consistently focused on the need of community and the change necessary so that the beauty of music can authentically announce the dawn of a better world.

As she looked back upon her life, Carolyn recalled with passion how movements have worked. She spoke of her desire to join her voice and her music to all authentic liberation movements — movements that free children, women, the young of Earth and the vulnerable of every species. She sings for all movements that believe that love turns us around and frees us. Carolyn also pointed out how capitalism and all systems of domination and competition stand in the way of a loving, celebratory context for life. More is possible—more inclusion, more forgiveness, more freedom, more peace, more diminishment of war and violence and more capacity to seek out a faith that is committed to touch each of us.

This magnificent soul of song reminded us that miracles happen in the common and simple events of our lives. She proclaimed to this gathering of seekers, "Behold, what we are about is one great possibility." Carolyn counseled that in the face of conflict and confrontation we remain in open conversation rather than depart and go away. With great wisdom, she reminded us that "violence and belittling of the other" will not work.

As Carolyn prepared to leave, she pondered that she wasn't certain what had happened among us, but she smiled and said, "Something tells me that it's good." And she suggested that we

- refrain from adversarial images.
- avoid blame and accusation of others.
- hold out a vision that touches each of us and will work miracles in the hearts of the young.
- appreciate and celebrate the beauty into which we are moving.

Carolyn invited us to experience through an unshielded heart, the very core of our being to create a world that is deeper, more affirming than before. As she stood at the piano one more time and responded to a final request to lead us in one of her signature songs, "O Beautiful Gaia," my thoughts meandered onto something Carolyn had said earlier, "I don't know what happened here but it will be with me the rest of my life."

Prophetic Voices

In the natural world, we discover the mysterious power whence all things come into being. (Thomas Berry)

God hugs you. You are encircled in the arms of the mystery of God. (Hildegarde of Bingen)

The deeper truths of our lives seem to need paradox for full expression. It is then we truly soar on wings of spirit. (Parker Palmer)

The most beautiful thing we can experience is the mysterious. (Albert Einstein)

If I had influence with the good fairy who is supposed to preside over the christening of all children, I should ask that her gift to each child in the world be a sense of wonder so indestructible that it would last throughout life. (Rachel Carson)

A Moment of Silence

Response: Expression of Mystery

Our journey is not to resist or justify, but rather to respond and pursue an authentic life. To accomplish this, we continue to explore those images, promptings and desires that draw us forward. Caught in a cosmic draft, we are continually drawn forward into a mysterious and unknown future as we move forward with passion and purpose.

Spend a few minutes in silent reflection on the Universe Story or one of the quotations above and then respond. How has mystery touched your life? Use poetry if you feel called to do so or perhaps express your response in a song, drawing or other art form that may come more easily than words.

Closing of the Day ~ The Universe Speaks of Mystery

~ Our lives are enveloped in mystery. Through mystery we encounter the Divine, the One who is beyond our experience yet simultaneously present in everything we see, feel, hear, taste and touch.

~ In the Monastery of the Cosmos we are invited to cross over the threshold and become engaged at the edge of mystery; from this place we enter a place of wonder that is without words or images or understanding; each incarnational moment is an encounter with the Divine.

~ Jon Sobrino writes: "The world of the poor places us before a mystery, and they themselves express mystery".

TUESDAY

DAWN

Theme: The Sacred

"Let your light shine among others that they may see your good works."

(Gospel of Matthew)

The Universe Story is more than a scientific account of evolution. The new story is a sacred story that reveals the mysterious presence of the Divine. Every molecule of existence, every flower, child and tree is soaked in the Divine. Each one is a moment of awe and wonder as our imaginations erupt, hearts open and spirits soar. When we open our lives to the Divine, we remember that we are here to resacralize the Earth. Wendell Berry writes, "To live we must daily break the body and shed the blood of creation...when we do it reverently, it is a sacrament."

Reflection: In Search of the Sacred

During my life the understanding of divinity has evolved and continues to do so. As a child, I attended a small white wooden mission church in Sombra, Ontario. The sanctuary for liturgy, named after John the Evangelist, was eventually blown over by the wind and now only a monument remains. I recall attending Mass there with my family as a child. I was told, "The pope is the head of the church." But Pope Pius XII seemed elusive. I was unable to find him in that creaking structure that swayed precariously in the breeze off the nearby St. Clare River.

As the years passed, my notion of God evolved. God became a hovering presence who would now and in the future pass judgment on my life and more particularly on my feelings. This idea of divinity inspired fear. This God seemed distant, way off in heaven and removed from my life. "He" governed and judged while comfort and love seemed far away.

The renewed energy released through the convoking of the Second Vatican Council made a life of faith more palpable. I participated in the Cursillo movement; this short course in Christianity brought meaning to the theological concepts that I was taught and made Christianity more accessible. I gave homilies entitled "Jesus as Our Brother;" the incarnation came home in my life. The poor and neglected became portraits of the suffering servant. Jesus lived among us, especially among the poor. The beatitudes became the central proclamation of the gospel. I now understand that my intent was to make God look like me.

My next step on the journey was the gift of the mystics who asserted that every atom is soaked in God — God is in all things and all things are in God. All life is sacred, not just the human, but also the daisy, puppy, brook and rain. This shift toward a world embedded in the sacred carried enormous implications. Not only are we called to feed the poor and the sick, but we also are here to restore and celebrate the beauty and rights of the rainforest, the oceans, the rocks and the soil. Suddenly, the call of the Christian took on a new perspective. Life became a seamless garment — the response to the poor and the poor Earth had become one act.

Today, I am only beginning to comprehend the implications of locating my life within this sacred and unfolding story. Interestingly, as I meditate and live my life within this new moment, the God of the small white mission church on the banks of the river now seems both personal and cosmic.

The God of the Cosmos has literally come down to Earth. I realize that all of life is mystery — to name and celebrate those moments is our challenge and privilege. The god of my childhood has transformed from a vague papal impression into an ineffable imageless presence in whom I believe but do not know. Yes, the God of the Cosmos has come down to Earth and is now that creative energy I dare to call my life.

Threshold Thoughts

Magnificat for the Stranger
Sacred sleepers
heal their tattered soul
as sounds of slumber
waft across the Tenderloin Cathedral

Travelers from our broken world
reweave their tapestry of life
journey toward the Promised Land
where no one is apart from me

A new Magnificat is sung
there are no strangers now
here at this barbecue of hope
we have seen the Promised Land

In the Deep Darkness
In the deep darkness
everything is seen
bugs, polliwogs
painful memories
and signs of hope.

What a wonderful sun-swept day
I land on this sea of life
on the edge of a precipice
I come to ponder
and gaze into the welcoming night
into the unseen dawn
the place of turbulence and hope.

I pray today and ask
what is heaven for?
what is the meaning of it all,
beauty, life, birth, death
and all the afterwards of the unexpected?
I ask all this
as the beetle walks across my arm.

Story: The Great Hunger

It was early Sunday morning when I was headed for the YMCA. As I rode my bike past the city post office, I noticed four teenagers lying on the steps, still tucked into their blankets and sleeping bags, not quite ready to get up and face another day. These homeless ones make us uncomfortable and yet touch us at our core. Their presence conjures up the child in us who longs for home. When frightened or alarmed "by people in the streets," remember it is a dimension of yourself that walks there, that lives without address and documented identity and perhaps spent last night in a "cardboard condo" in a park, a storefront or the rain.

My brief encounter with these four people reminded me of the biblical story of the multiplication of the loaves and fishes, a story of hunger and great abundance. I thought of the thirty-three percent of the world's population that had gone to bed hungry last night and the thousands of children who would die of hunger today. I recalled the famines that have ravaged so many lands throughout history and the deep hunger that affected my own ancestors a century and a half ago when their crops failed in Ireland. Again I pondered the story of the loaves and fishes while I witnessed these homeless ones asleep on the steps of the Berkeley post office. How can this happen in a society where overeating fuels a multi-billion dollar weight-loss industry!

Later, an immense pathos of hunger and homelessness flooded my consciousness. Is the reason that we as a culture feel incapable of housing the homeless and feeding the hungry because we ourselves are starved—starved for an experience that can strengthen our souls and nourish our hearts? If we could satisfy our deep desire for the Divine and feel at home in the Universe, would we not then have the inner abundance to house and feed those in need? I have a deep conviction that the answer is yes—and that the answer is love.

Prophetic Voices

What is Divine? It is the ineffable pervasive presence in the world about us. (Thomas Berry)

The difficulty is that the natural world is seen primarily for human use, not as made of sacred presence primarily to be communed with in wonder and beauty and intimacy ... a sacred reality to be venerated. (Thomas Berry)

All creation is a symphony of joy and jubilation. (Hildegarde of Bingen)

Blessed be you, mighty matter, irresistible march of evolution, reality ever newborn; you who, by constantly shattering our mental categories, force us to go ever further and further in our pursuit of truth. (Pierre Teilhard de Chardin)

Beauty comes to us with no work of our own, then leaves us prepared to undergo a great labor. (Elaine Scarry)

Perhaps the greatest progress, human speaking, in these past twenty years is the growth of consciousness...a new consciousness of our place in the universe, and a new awareness of the interrelatedness of all life on our planet. (Anne Morrow Lindbergh)

A Moment of Silence

Response: Life as Sacred

The invitation today is to recognize that all matter is holy. Teilhard de Chardin underlines this when he writes, "The flesh was made Word." The sacred is soaked in the Divine. The words of the medieval mystic, Mechtild of Magdenburg, captures our imagination of the Universe as Divine embodiment, "On the day of my spiritual awakening, I saw and knew that I saw God in all things. All Things in God." Notice yourself when you reverence Earth and her people from this perspective.

> Heal me, Holy One. Take me to the portal of pure potentiality. Transport me over the doorway of struggle to new life and through the canal of unlimited possibilities to know again that which seemed apparently lost. Where freedom reigns, where all fragmentation heals, we are taken up, enveloped by membranes of mystery, wrapped in wonder, bathed in beauty, embraced by belonging. Sacredness happens and uncertainties fade away.

As you take in these words, is there something that springs forth within you? Manifest your response in word, sound, movement or silence.

DUSK

Theme: The Sacred

"You will learn more in the woods than you will in books. The trees and stones will teach you what you never learn in the schools of the masters." (St. Bernard)

We experience the sacred when we understand that the Divine is present within the natural world, permeating all things including the human, mammals, lizards and frogs, fish and flora, bacteria and minerals, water, air, soil, sunlight. Every expression is Earth. From this inclusive perspective all matter is holy. God is not distant from the world but resides within it.

Reflection: Singing the Song of Nature

Concern for nature and our natural systems is relatively recent in the world of culture and spirituality. The word ecology, the relation of life with one another, was not even in the common vocabulary when I was in college. However, the ravages inflicted upon our planet by the industrial age have now impressed the fragility of Earth upon the human conscience. A new awareness has formed about our interrelatedness and interconnection with all creation.

Today, ecology speaks of the sacred web or circle of life; it reminds us that each action, each breath, is connected to everything else. Chief Seattle writes: "Every part of this earth is sacred...all things are connected...whatever we do to the web we do to ourselves." Ecology is how we look at our interrelated world. In its most profound sense ecology is about Earth, our sacred home, and our responsibility for the habitat and well being of all species. It is about relationship, interaction and open dialogue.

Nature reminds us that all life is a unique expression of the Divine. Liberation theologian Leonardo Boff describes ecology as "the science and art of relationship and related beings."

Story: Boy at the Park

It was late afternoon on a hot summer day in Oakland. Young children of West Oakland had spent the day at a city park. They played games in the soft grass, swam in the pool and gazed at the birds above as they ate their lunch under the shade of a great oak whose stately presence adorned the park. Moments later, the counselors reminded the children that it was time to board the bus to return to their neighborhood, an area that is best described as an asphalt jungle. As he entered the bus, a little boy cried inconsolably. When asked what was wrong, he blurted out, "I don't want to leave my park!" As he took his seat for the ride home, it was evident that boy had been touched by the sacredness of the natural world.

Link to the Beginning

A little boy, about four years old, is playing upstairs in his parents' room. Suddenly he calls out in excitement to his mother downstairs. He has found the family bible. He turns the pages and finds a maple leaf that has been pressed within the pages. With great wonder the little boy shouts out, "Momma, I think I have found Adam's underwear!"

Threshold Thoughts

The Songs of the Sacred
With gratitude and grace
we celebrate the story
of creation, liberation and us

in blessing and brokenness
we restore hunger for newness
boiling from the wellsprings of our souls
here within wonder and surprise
we rediscover hope
and recognize once more the signature of God

Sun shines on my window
sparrows chirp "hello"
rain arrives from heaven
earth radiates new life

Everywhere a world that's sacred
makes proclamations to the sky
while from within the heart of all creation
revelation announces a fond "hello"

Energetic patterns
tell of all our stories
while the inner search
echoes deep within

We awaken to the crises and causes of our time
and find within the deep wells of tradition
connections to the unstopped cosmic river
that is the oceanic source of our God

The Cricket Becomes a Scribe
What is a poem?
perhaps an insight into life
a felt sense of the sacred
a conviction about
what needs to be done?

Does the robin write in rhymes?
Is the rhinoceros a bard?

Do clouds inscribe the sky?
Is not each sunrise a poem
every rainfall a sonnet
morning glories heralds of the day?

You don't know a poem
until your heart leaps
and you love the little ones
when the cricket on the back porch
becomes a scribe

Prophetic Voices

Contemplation is life itself. It is spiritual wonder. It is spontaneous awe at the sacredness of life. It is gratitude for life, for awareness, and for being. (Thomas Merton)

Let us give thanks for the web and the circle that connects us. Thanks be to God. The God of All! (Chief Seattle)

Go to the earth...and ask it for guidance. Let yourself go and let God be in you. (Meister Eckhart)

Look deep into nature and then you will understand everything better. (Albert Einstein)

It is spring again. The earth is like a child that knows poems by heart. (Rainer Maria Rilke)

A wrong attitude toward nature implies, somewhere, a wrong attitude toward God. (T.S. Eliot)

Protect the earth. It was not given to you by your parents; it is lent to you by your children. (Kenyan song)

A thing is right when it tends to preserve the integrity, stability and beauty of the biotic community. It is wrong when it tends otherwise. (Aldo Leopold)

God is the most beautiful thing there is. (Francis of Assisi)

Whenever we awaken beauty, we are helping to make God present in the world. (John O'Donohue)

A Moment of Silence

Response: Sacred Dialogue

Within each of us there is an unquenchable quest for the sacred. We long to connect the experience of nature and everyday life to a world replete with meaning and purpose. Throughout my life, I have journeyed with others and have found ways to touch divinity and explore its implications for our lives. We have searched for a common language, one that names the dynamics of our existence — Meister Eckhart names it, "Isness is God" and "Just to be is Holy" — and provides a context that allows us to ask the enduring questions:

- How do we authentically live our relationship with Earth?
- How do we intimately communicate with the Divine?
- How can we best fulfill the reason for our existence?
- Why are there challenges, obstacles and suffering to confront us?

Reflect on these incessant questions. Express your reflection in image, words, sound or movement.

Closing of the Day ~ The Universe Speaks of the Sacred

~ Our lives, in fact the entire Universe, is infused with the sacred; the Divine permeates every molecule of existence.

~ The experience of the sacred takes us to a portal of unlimited possibilities, a doorway to new life where fragmentation heals, where beauty shines forth. Our spirit soars and divinity is palpably present everywhere.

~ A place of wonder that dilates the soul and the connective tissue of belonging weaves a tapestry of inclusiveness and new life.

~ We become grateful and energized to play our role in the Great Work of our generation where fullness happens and uncertainties fade away.

WEDNESDAY

DAWN

Theme: The Human

"May the God of peace furnish you with all that is good." (Letter to the Hebrews)

"Good people produce goodness from the good they store up in their hearts... People speak from the fullness of their hearts." (Gospel of Luke)

From the beginning humanity is integral with the Universe. Full humanity is realized when each person achieves the fullest expression of his or her gifts. When each individual gives himself or herself to the care and love of Earth, their lives will deepen and their destinies realized.

Reflection: A Listening Heart

The StoryCorps: Recording America project is the largest independent oral history movement in the United States. Thousands of people have participated as they listen, laugh and recollect the stories of their lives. The core of the project is the conversation between two people who are important to each other. The intent is to record and preserve the personal stories of a person important to them. These stories throw a light on the courage, humor, struggles, celebrations and grace that illuminates the individual's life. When others hear these ordinary yet inspirational stories, they are moved into the knowing "of just how precious each day can be and how truly great it is to be alive." The powerful experience of StoryCorps both as participant and listener exemplifies the practice of a listening heart. By listening closely to one another, we are saying that life matters.

The heart is the home of wisdom. As we listen deeply, we hear in our hearts the silent ancient call that summons a newfound source of strength, continuity and courage. When we tell our story, we experience strength in the face of uncertainty; continuity when hope is not always evident; courage when life appears to be slipping away; vision in a world where darkness too often holds sway. We laugh and cry and celebrate our life. Through storytelling the heart-focus shifts from accomplishment to contemplation, from going out to going within.

Moving into deep listening of the these stories allows for an inner shift filled with wondrous treasures — rich ancestral memories can open us to a fresh appreciation of the past and a clarifying direction for the future. Sometimes, suddenly it often seems, we find that the artifacts of our ancestors fascinate us. The old family clock hanging on the wall takes on new meaning. More now than a timepiece, it becomes a living reminder, a story announcing itself from the bedroom. Cemeteries become narratives of families, maps of lineage stretching into former times, bringing forth cherished memories and an activated appreciation of the past. Birthdays and anniversaries announce the endless march of time as we remember and savor past moments. Story is remembering — by listening to story, we honor and celebrate the lives of our ancestors and ourselves.

Threshold Thoughts

The Descent
What holds us together?
how is the pond, dandelion and turtle one?
where is the cosmic glue?
is it Jesus on the road to Emmaus?
the breeze that hovers from the sky
who made the wind?
who made the desire to be one?

is it not the cosmic one
the pattern that connects us all
come now everyone
commune with all creation
join the mystery of all

New Light
Clouds part
day arrives

Tomorrow looks brighter now
life's limits have a kinder look

Cosmic return
becomes a peaceful view

Embrace what's real
be at peace

In the darkness of despair shine the light of faith
penetrate the terrible isolation with illumination
a spark of possibility

O holy one, heal the wounded world; the heart beats
frantically on the killing fields of war and in the
heart of every mother's newborn child

Go deeply into the dark
embrace the hand of hope
stay strong in the face of fear

Shine with compassion into this dark night
bring peace to my soul and to all who tremble
in the dark

Story: Mary, My Sister

Mary was born on a beautiful spring day in Port Lambton, Ontario. She was an intelligent child, her parents' pride and joy, who excelled in school. Mary went on to do her graduate work at Columbia University where she taught for some time. Eventually, taking a high-level position at Mobil Oil, she broke the glass ceiling with her many accomplishments, that included being the first female economist hired by the corporation. Yet, what is most remarkable about Mary is that she stayed rooted in her family, her ancestral values and the local communities in which she lived.

Following her early retirement, Mary's generosity actively expressed itself in many ways, including twenty-plus years of volunteer service at the local food bank. One day, when asked why she chose to give her many gifts to the food bank, she replied, "My ancestors suffered from the famine in Ireland and I want to do something to feed the hungry."

My sister served as the family archivist and genealogical expert, tracking down ancestors in Ireland and France as well as touring the farms, homes and cemeteries of our French and Irish relatives within our homeland of Ontario, Canada. On one occasion we Canadian Conlons stood together in a cemetery in Ireland with fifteen other Conlons from overseas to honor our ancestral roots. At another reunion Mary generously shared her genealogical findings with the Conlon family at the community center in the village of Sombra where she was raised.

Mary Olive Conlon is a woman of graciousness and faith, a good friend to many and a loving relative to all the Conlons. When I look at Mary's life, I see a living scripture in action that challenges each of us to live fully. She is a gift to the world, a true blessing to the Conlons and a dear sister to me.

Prophetic Voices

Violation of the individual is a violation of the community. (Thomas Berry)

The poet needs the practicalities of making a living to test and temper the lyricism of insight and observation. The composition needs the poet's insight and power with attention in order to weave the inner world of soul creativity with the outer world with form and matter. (David Whyte)

A richly elaborated life connected to society and nature, woven into the culture of family, nature and globe. (Thomas Moore's description of "soulwork")

Poetry is prayer, it is passion and story and music, it is beauty, comfort, it is agitation, dedication, it is thanksgiving…Some poems are radiant and oracular, some are quiet and full of tenderness, like a letter written to a friend. Often poetry is the gate to a new life. (Mary Oliver)

Moment of Silence

Response: Conscious Self-Reflection

Imagine that moment in time when our human ancestor looked out into the world, then looked back upon herself, and then looked at herself looking out into the world. What a transformational moment! In that split second, an enormous leap of self and self within the larger context was brought into existence. Conscious self-reflection was born, evolving humanity to the next level. But oh, what a frightening exquisite moment that must have been for that one human! And when she returned to her community, how did she explain such a thing to the others?

Contemplate for a few moments the cosmological power that has made it possible for humanity to reflect on itself. Stay with this realization for a few minutes and then express your response in words, images or sound.

DUSK

Theme: The Human

We humans cannot live in dignity and freedom while we pollute our planetary home. (Diarmuid O'Murchu)

We are a people of the Great Work called to liberate and transform both humans and our planet. Content, but never satisfied, we listen deeply with the ear of the heart. Ever so conscious of our limitations, yet grounded in the wondrous beauty of this land, we approach the precipice of new beginnings and take the vow of risk. Moved on by precious companions, we unearth a renewed commitment to do whatever needs to be done — we say Yes to the unknown future.

Reflection: Deep Desire

Some have described today's society as a culture without vocation. As a people, we are without a deep sense of purpose, identity or destiny. Many things contribute to this. Young people often have little confidence in the future. Employment opportunities are limited and many people are forced to settle for low-paying jobs without much hope for challenging work or advancement. At the same time, advertising emphasizes immediate gratification. And why not, since life seems temporary and unsure. This view of life, in turn, further militates against commitment to long-term career preparation and goals that require delayed gratification.

In an era of turbulence and transition, alienation abounds; people feel disconnected from family, Earth and themselves. This futile sense of insatiable hunger and homelessness echoes our primary loss – our separation from Earth. Everywhere I go I sense the hunger for a calling, a vocation. People experience a deep desire to be in touch with the Mystery that continues to call us into life—whether they can articulate this longing clearly or not.

My own deepest desire always has been to be who I am supposed to be and to live my life for the purpose it was intended. I want to live fully, with generosity and gratitude, striving to break new ground and not always to follow the paths others have blazed. As I live my moment of the Universe Story, I pray daily for the wisdom to see the beauty, wonder and belonging all around me.

Threshold Thoughts

Song of the Sandinistas
High Perches/Low Aspirations
isolated people
sitting on high stools
seemingly espousing
low aspirations
for their lives
gazing into a silver tube
belching out the venom
of a failed leadership
of a previously promised land
from these high perches
unreflected awareness
seems to ooze from somewhere
and spill into an ever-darkening room

Story: Almost Nothing

Sister Jan spent many years in Guatemala. Now living in Milwaukee, her dedication to the Central American peoples continues as she regularly takes groups to experience the culture, meet the people and listen to their stories.

On one occasion Sister Jan was in El Salvador with a group from the United States. One day her group was introduced to some local citizens from El Salvador. One of the Salvadorans was a young girl, perhaps ten years old, named Anna.

A man from the group posed a question to the girl, "What do you love most about living in El Salvador?"

Her answer came back, "Almost nothing."

The bleak honesty of her reply startled him, shook him to his core. As a result of his brief but poignant encounter with this little girl, the man took upon himself the task of raising money to bring clear and fresh water to that region of El Salvador.

Hope for the Future

We have come to a new moment, a turning point, a defining time in our personal and collective journey. This realization came home to me as I listened to the story of an elderly Nicaraguan woman who lived in the rural area of her Central American country. This woman stood proudly by the site where a new school would be built. She was asked, "Can you read?" With a gentle, knowing smile she responded, "Not yet."

Prophetic Voices

The human emerges within the life systems of earth as that being in whom the universe reflects on and celebrates itself in a special mode of conscious self-expression. The human is genetically coded toward a further cultural coding. (Thomas Berry)

Serious people of faith need to return to the center, to the inmost core that alone can nourish and warm the heart. (Elizabeth Johnston)

The human psyche is essentially commensurate with the whole universe. (Stan Grof)

Poets are most profoundly in communion with other modes of understanding. (Thomas Berry)

God speaks to us and walks with us...I feel it now...There is a power in me to grasp and give shape to the world. (Rainer Maria Rilke)

Where shall we find that vital impulse, that soul, let us say that fullness of spirit? ...This is the hour of the poor, of the millions of poor who are everywhere on the earth. (Cardinal Lercaro, Vatican Council II)

Moment of Silence

Response: The New Cosmology

Cosmology, according to the American Heritage Dictionary, is "the study of the physical universe considered as a totality of phenomena in time and space," i.e., the origin of the Universe, its unfolding in time and the human's place in the process. The new cosmology is the scientific story of evolution of the Universe, born 13.7 billion years ago from a pinpoint explosion of mega-intense heat and energy. Like a broken cosmic egg, all life flowed forth, establishing the foundation of our physical universe, namely, hydrogen and helium. From these early gases flowed the galaxies and their billions of stars, our Sun and solar system, Earth and all her life forms. Everything in the Universe was born in that single microsecond; everything in our Universe shares the same roots; everything is part of the great expansion that moves into greater complexity, diversity and beauty.

The indigenous peoples of Earth intuitively knew this story; it is only in the last five hundred years that western civilization has been able to scientifically begin to tell and detail this mythic narrative. The beauty of the unfolding story of the Universe is that it holds the overarching truth of total inclusivity. The new cosmology makes sense out of the senseless, gives understanding and meaning to our lives and eternally yields to a Universe of mystery. Every moment is dipped in awe and wonder.

What then does it mean to be a cosmological being, a citizen of the cosmos? How do you begin to grasp the holiness and wholeness in this story? What difference does that make in your life? How does this vision make you more fully human? Perhaps a nonverbal meditation through song, art, dance, movement or simple silence is the most appropriate response here.

Closing of the Day ~ The Universe Speaks of the Human

~ Humanity is integral with the Universe from the beginning and fully realized when each person achieves the fullest expression of his or her gifts. We are today challenged to create community where everyone is included.

~ We are a people of the Great Work called to liberate and transform both people and the planet. Content, but never satisfied, we listen deeply with the "ear of the heart" and move forward to create a context where beauty, wonder and belonging can shine forth.

~ From the far reaches of the cosmos and the deepest recesses of our souls, we move forward to contemplate what it means to be human in this transitional moment in human/Earth history. As we shift the focus from accomplishment to contemplation, we, with childlike curiosity, approach the precipice of new beginnings and take the vow of risk at this liminal moment of an as yet unknown future.

THURSDAY

DAWN

Theme: This Moment

"Our one desire is that each of you show the same zeal to the end, to the perfect fulfillment of our hopes." *(Letter to the Hebrews)*

Each person was chosen to live at this historic moment, our moment in the Universe. The spiritual journey calls us forward and challenges us to meet each moment as an opportunity for hope to participate and play our part to bring justice and fulfillment to our time. To live in the moment requires a personal decision, the kind of decision that brings about a change of heart and sustains a long-term commitment.

Reflection: Cosmic Resurrection

Theologically, what is happening is nothing less than the intense and critical reenactment of the paschal mystery, the ongoing incarnation of death and resurrection in our present moment. We are called to think, pray and reflect theologically about our place and response. We must not merely cope; we must exercise capable, creative and competent leadership.

We think. Through contemplation we deepen our spiritual journey. We see that what we most deeply believe is rooted in our tradition. We have an increased conviction that the Divine permeates all of life, and that reverencing creation for its own sake is in fact an act of faith.

Strengthened by this awareness, we can explore its implications for our lives and for Earth. As we reflect on our experiences in the light of faith, we search for resources that will increase our capacity to respond. We are invited to think about science, from which all peoples receive a common story of Earth; about our faith, which perceives Earth as God's unique creation; and about our work, which is born in our hearts and minds from the needs of Earth.

We pray. Prayer, in the context of geo-justice, consists of keeping our hearts and minds open to the beauty and the crises of our time. We listen so that we can respond creatively and courageously.

We reflect theologically. To create an operative theology, we need to discover what of our inherited traditions most deeply influence our action in the world. For example, the Inuit people of the Northwest Territories hold hospitality as a primary cornerstone of their faith tradition, for it is a most prefound value to basic survival. Making these connections releases enormous energy and enables us to contribute more fully to healing Earth.

Threshold Thoughts

Matins on a Dark Day
Despair is a dreadful path
sinking into darkness
without things to hope for
or pride in what's been done

Do weeping willows cry
are cattle sheltered in the storm sad
do the bleeding heart in the garden cause
beauty and pain?

Cheer up proclaims
the morning glory
as all creation chants
matins to Earth

Home to Life
Is the cloud lonely
resting in the sky on high?

What about the bluebird
perched stately in the great oak?

Or the grasshopper who stands
alert on the lawn?

Realize we all belong
come home to life

Story: A Stellar View

It was a cold, crisp night in early December. A full moon hung like a great yellow lantern in the late autumn sky. When clouds parted, the moon was visible in radiant splendor. When the clouds reappeared, this lunar spectacle was hidden and it was time to wait for the next burst of light.

A small child became fascinated by this cosmic drama in the dark night. He took his mother by the hand and led her over to the window to watch. There they sat together, looking into the night. When the clouds parted and the moon shone through, the child shook with joyful exuberance at such a stellar view.

As the mother embraced her son by the window that evening, she wondered, "Is this not the first time I have really seen the moon?"

Judy Cannato shared this story when she visited the Sophia Center to lead a weekend program on the themes of her best selling book, *Radical Amazement.* The story of how her son played peek-a-boo with the moon is a vivid illustration of the awe and wonder accessible to each of us in and through the night sky.

Prophetic Voices

We must be at the heart of things, of life, present where the future is in the process of being born, participating in its creation. (Jean Marie Elia)

To become at the same time and by the same act, one with all through release from all multiplicity or material gravity. There you have, deeper than any ambition for place, for wealth or power, the dream of the human soul. (Pierre Teilhard de Chardin)

You must give birth to your images. They are the future waiting to be born. The future must enter into you long before it happens. (Rainer Maria Rilke)

Moment of Silence

Response: The Call of Your Time

The call to meaningful mysticism is a summons to reenergize your capacity for God—a capacity that transcends restlessness, woundedness, the ego and the tendency toward negativity. It is a call into right relationship with the Divine, Earth and all her beings. It is being accountable for your thoughts and actions while you live as a responsible, trustworthy member of the Earth community.

It is heeding the words that what we do to the least of us, we do to ourselves. This moment in time is not for the weak, spineless or faint-hearted. Rather, it is your unique moment in the sun to rise to your true potential of being fully human. Clarissa Pinkola Estes counsels us, "You were born for this time." Thomas Berry reminds us, "You were chosen."

Take some time to ponder your place in the great unfolding mystery of this moment. What is your role and your response? Our endangered planet awaits your response. Through word, image, movement or sound, give expression to your response to this present moment.

DUSK

Theme: This Moment

"All great transcendental moments are sacrificial moments. Our present transition will not be accomplished without enormous sacrifice. Our hope is that the work we are doing, demanding as it is, is succeeding, and that we are on our way to a grand, celebratory place of the earth, of life, of the human community—a new place in the story of the universe." (Thomas Berry)

We are witnessing the coming into being of a moment that will mark the end of an era and the beginning of something new. We enter a shifting paradigm, an era marked by the deepest aspiration of the human heart, which is motivated by the realization and conviction that our lives are founded in original goodness. As we witness the collapse of the American empire, and as other institutions retreat from relevance, we proclaim the Now as the era of the new human.

Reflection: Enveloped in this Moment

Life unfolds in wondrous and unpredictable ways. As we search for meaning, we stand alert and listen to the wisdom constantly proclaimed by hearts, voices, trees, meadows, rivers and creatures who at first seem to say nothing. They "speak" a pulsating rhythm, a proclamation, a divine whisper that consoles, challenges, comforts and proclaims. Earth speaks and all creation calls our name. We listen deeply to the uninterrupted yet wordless proclamation that the God of the cosmos has come home to Earth.

Our spiritual journey can be understood as departure and return. Our lives begin with a certain level of naiveté and innocence —mysticism and creativity is the authentic legacy of each person.

Yet, we find our lives framed and confined by our ancestral roots and the traditions and cultures in which we were raised.

The spiritual journey involves a departure from the framework of our pasts. To embark courageously on this important and profound adventure requires the practice of detachment—detachment from past practices and beliefs. The journey asks us to be open and courageous to meet the shattering of our limited worldview. As we search for our new identity, at least for the moment we let go of the old, trusting that a more mature, foundational spirituality will emerge. This inclusive emergent spirituality seeks to return us to the mysticism and creativity of the child while retaining the sacred wisdom available at the heart of other world traditions.

From this personal experience of deconstruction and creation will flow a spirituality that is ancient and new, naive and seasoned, childlike and mature, rooted in our origins and the practices of sacred traditions of the past.

Threshold Thoughts

The Promise
Arise from rubble
from depths
awake to power

In this new moment
make time
to heal
from pain and devastation

Arise tender ones
awake to our new moment

Welcome the dawn
thank the morning
greet with gratitude
the promise of today

Wake up glad
at dawn
to the great tabernacle of mystery
at dusk

Story: Peace in the Wilderness

It was a late evening in Baghdad. The night was full of flashes of light as bombs fell from the sky, announcing the onset of "Iraqi freedom." Almost unaware of the danger, a group of children played a game though the time was late.

Kathy Kelly, founder of Voices in the Wilderness, a Chicago-based peace group, urged the children to complete their game because it was their bedtime. In a unified response to her urging, the children protested in one voice, "But Miss, we may not be here in the morning."

As the bombs continued to fall, the children finally went off to bed. I'm sure they wondered, as do I, why can't they play in peace? Why is our world so torn and tattered? As they played and slept that evening, the children were a voice in the wilderness for all who seek the true meaning of peace.

Intergenerational Magic

While I was in Milwaukee, I visited an innovative project called An Intergenerational Center. One side of the facility is a day-care center for adults, many of them burdened with physical challenges and developmental disabilities. The other side is a day-care for children from the ages of six-months to school age.

Each day the older children cross the floor of the building to visit the adults. Both tell and share stories, laugh, play and enjoy one another's company. The result is magic! Both the adults and children emerge from these daily interactions with vitality and vibrancy, beauty and fresh energy. A zest for life shines through their eyes.

We are made for this task. We can all contribute to setting free the captives of our day, including our fragile blue planet.

Prophetic Voices

My heart is moved by all I cannot change. So much is being destroyed. I have cast my lot with those who age after age perversely and with no extraordinary power reconstitute the world. (Adrienne Rich)

He will never waiver nor be crushed until justice is established on earth. (Isaiah)

Vocation does not come from willfulness. It comes from listening. It means a calling that I hear. (Parker Palmer)

I don't know who or what put the questions. I don't even know when it was put. I don't even remember answering. But at some point I did answer "yes" to someone or something. And from that hour I was certain that existence was meaningful and therefore my life was self-surrendered and whole. (Dag Hammarskjöld)

But I always think that the best way to know God is to love many things. (Vincent Van Gogh)

Moment of Silence

Response: Sacred Promptings

Our spiritual journey invites us to evoke the courage and creativity necessary to find our voice, incarnate our gifts and stand steadfast in the storms of life. Grounded within the silence of our heart, we approach each new day with an attitude that is content but not satisfied. From within our journey sacred promptings emerge that create opportunities to put our vision into action.

How do you understand your vision at this moment? How do you feel called to put your vision into action? What is the connection between your spiritual practice and your engagement in the world? Compose a list of strategies and tactics that will help you put your vision into action.

Closing of the Day ~ The Universe Speaks of This Moment

~ We live at a defining moment in human/Earth history. To be prepared for this moment will require that we excavate our consciousness; to discover deep wells of solitude, heal the maladies and obsessions of our addictive culture and re-energize our capacity for God.

~This new moment invites us to transcend restlessness, woundology and a tendency to complain; to retrieve our lost identity and allow the true self to shine through the diamond of spiritual experience.

~ We awaken to a vast realization that this is our moment in the Universe story.
~ An incarnation is a moment, a place where hope happens and we experience the divine as we follow the compass of the heart.
~ At this new moment we envision a world where every voice is heard, every position welcomed and every plan considered as we celebrate the universality of change, realizing that we were born for these time.

FRIDAY

DAWN

Theme: Struggle and Fulfillment

"Let kindness and loyalty never leave you. Tie them round your neck; write them in the tablet of your heart." (Book of Proverbs)

The spiritual journey invites us to find fulfillment — discover the Divine — in the midst of our struggle. Each moment of struggle can be seen as an opportunity to heal the planet and ourselves, and through acts of transformation more fully realize our purpose and destiny. As Mary Oliver says: "I tell you this to break your heart. To break your heart open that it never again be closed to the world."

Reflection: An Urban Contemplative

Many people today can appropriately be called urban contemplatives. They often feel dislocated from the ebb and flow of everyday existence, awash in a world of misguided mysticism. These are seekers who painfully experience a propagandized media that is focused on the casualties of war and the latest closing results of the stock market.

Urban contemplatives feel the pain of disconnection and apparent defensiveness in a world that seems to have decided not to listen. They are hungry for meaning and purpose as they search daily in a society at odds with itself. They feel a deep and enduring impulse to penetrate the clouds of illusion and isolation that surround their lives.

Urban contemplatives hear the voice of Teilhard beckoning them to descend into the inmost self and discover the "wellspring that they dare to call their life."

They listen to the guidance of Thomas Berry, who reminds them that the God of the cosmos is present in every blade of grass urging us to commune with the healing beauty of the natural world.

They hear Thomas Merton's call to the contemplative life, a call to the true self, that "virgin point" where we encounter in a transparent way the divine presence that lies at the heart of the Universe and in the deepest recesses of our soul.

As these people pursue with greater and greater intensity their call, urban contemplatives experience increased alienation from society and the events of daily life. Yet, within the depths of their souls, clarity appears and healing happens.

In many ways urban contemplatives represent all of our struggles and longings for an experience of the Divine. They seek a spirituality that supports their authentic within the self as well as within the Universe. Through lyrical language today's urban contemplatives search for words and images to name and share their experience. Their struggle is for an integration of inner clarity and outer engagement. It is here that urban contemplatives imbibe the sacredness of life.

Thomas Berry names the experience well when he writes: "The natural world is seen primarily for human use not as a mode of sacred presence primarily to be communed with in beauty, wonder, and intimacy… Only a sense of the sacred will save us."

I would add that only when the engaged urban contemplative comes home to God and to Earth will the "misfit" become a mystic.

Threshold Thoughts

Unbelief I
Help my unbelief
cried Thomas

There are so many wounds
to touch today
so many doubts and fears

So many questions not yet asked
so many answers not yet given

Who is God?
why am I here?
does suffering bring us life?
is there a purpose to it all?
is my choice a tragic mistake?

Today there are so many wounds
to pierce our hands
wounds of war, of death
of dreams unrealized
hopes dashed

In a world shaken by uncertainty
permeated by bitterness and pain
help my unbelief
give me hope and strength and perseverance
grant me invisible one
hope and peace

Unbelief II
Ancient One of ancient days
where are you now?
help my unbelief

Incarnate One
reveal your presence
help my unbelief

Pattern that connects us all
help my unbelief
Let me feel your presence
in the stars, sand and sea

Gather the fragments of our planetary soul
heal our fractured world

Let doubt subside
may the sun become each
morning a beacon of new life
to quench our thirst for wonder in the night

Oh Ineffable One
teach me rest and peace
the gratitude of presence
joy of embrace
and in the midst of so much doubt
trust my unbelief
in each new celestial moment

Hope bursts forth
unbidden and unseen
to quench the darkness of the night

Story: Remembering Joe

When the news came, I was saddened and relieved — sad that someone so loved and with such a large, eloquent heart had left us yet relieved that his long journey of pain had come to a peaceful end.

Joe was a man of noble spirit, joyful humor and deep compassion. He was someone that I, like so many others, was honored to call my friend. We were seminarians together during the turbulent years of the Vatican II Council. It was there that his hometown "Chatsworth" stories earned him the well-deserved reputation as a storyteller of wisdom, depth and many humorous tales. These stories were a gift he graciously shared throughout his life with anyone willing to listen and learn.

Our friendship flourished when Joe and I began our weekly journeys to communication therapy in Toronto. I remember joining Joe and a group of his friends when he decided to pursue the position at the Lakeshore Area Multi Service Project (LAMP). This is a social services umbrella that pulls together and coordinates the many local agencies for easier community access. This was a great choice; Joe's many gifts as community builder, communicator, celebrator and appreciator allowed the project to thrive. Both he and the project received recognition locally and beyond.

Perhaps my most cherished memory of Joe is the day that he and Susan became husband and wife. In recent years, although separated by miles, I was constantly moved by the deep affection and respect they had for each other and the way their widening circle of friends were always included within their special bond. The periodic updates from Susan during Joe's illness were much more than a medical report. These were love letters from

Susan to Joe that she generously shared with each of their close friends and family.

Joe's humor, compassion and love of life will never be forgotten. He taught me many lessons – how to love, how to laugh and how to endure life's burdens. May he rest in peace. Good by, dear friend.

Prophetic Voices

The damaged earth, violent and unjust structures, the lonely and broken hearted—all cry out for a fresh start. (Elizabeth Johnston)

We live in a state of semi-attention to the sound of voices, music, traffic, or generalized noise in what goes on all around us all the time…what we have to discover is our original unity. What we have to be is what we are. (Thomas Merton)

Our fate and future are also one. (Sallie McFague)

We are a people grasping for a renewed sense of place and community. (Barry Lopez)

There is no point at which we will say our work is finished. (Rachel Carson)

Lord . . . when I speak to the fox, the sparrow, the lost dog, the shivering sea-goose, know that really I am speaking to you whenever I say, as I do all morning and afternoon, Come in, Come in. (Mary Oliver)

Moment of Silence

Response: Eyes on Justice

When we read the Gospels carefully, we realize that Jesus makes reference to two types of Christians: the institutional and the kingdom, that is, those who follow the letter of the law and those who put others and Earth first through acts of compassion and empowerment.

The kingdom people are motivated by the chambers of the heart; their lives spring forth from the center of their sacredness. These are the people whose sacred hearts have been broken open by the pain of the world and the inevitable burdens of their lives. These people, with their broken hearts, become a healing presence; their expressions of compassion and love gather the fragments of our endangered planet. Through them, the gospel comes alive. These people, many of whom feel like refugees from their roots, become bridge builders between the ancient and the new. They live their lives enveloped in the vernacular of the day, yet feel rooted in and empowered by the wisdom of those who have gone before. Together they move forward with courage and resilience to transform the world, to offer compassion, to calm the troubled waters of our multi-tasking, anxious, accelerated culture.

How many times have we heard it said that life is not about winning, rather it's about the struggle? Czech poet and political leader Vaclav Havel reminds us that hope comes from doing what is worthwhile; it is not about success. What things have you done or have touched your life that have made you feel worthwhile? Ponder for a moment the struggles of your life. How can your life be fulfilled as you explore your response to your personal struggles?

DUSK

Theme: Struggle and Fulfillment

"When the heart breaks open, it can hold the whole universe." (Joanna Macy)

The practice of justice forms the centerpiece of the spiritual journey. This is a process of prayer, critical reflection and compassionate action to heal and transform the world.

Reflection: The Darkness

The mystery of the seasons and the rhythm of night and day enchant me. The darkness is a particular mystery. For me, it contains the frightening, the hidden, the unexpected.

John of the Cross wrote about what he called "the dark night of the soul". This expression seems particularly apt when my accomplishments seem only an illusion; when I lie awake at night dreading the morning and wondering if it will ever come; when existence seems meaningless.

Spiritual guides over the years teach that the primary response to these dark nights is not to fight them but to go deeply into the experience while at the same time taking good care of ourselves. Morning will come. The dark night does not last forever, and eventually light will dispel the darkness. We will emerge feeling cleansed of false perceptions. Our false ego will be re-formed, and our true self will emerge.

Cultures can experience a dark night too. As collapse and devastation proliferate around us, we must surrender our pathological way of life and seek out a new vision. The legacy of

John of the Cross is a particular gift as we struggle with these defining moments at the beginning of the third millennium. Perhaps it is true that the darkest hour is before dawn. If so, we have much to let go of and much for which to hope. Morning will come. Ours is a time of renaissance and rebirth.

Threshold Thoughts

Prayers to an Unknown God
Turmoil surfaces
past pain
has another face
memories singe my soul
lacerations of the psyche
become an open wound

Yet I hear another voice
Yes we can
fired up
audacity of hope
fierce urgency of Now

Ask not …
nothing to fear
I have a dream
Rosa took a seat
Martin marched
Jesse ran
Barack won

Blessed unrest
radical freedom
blue gold
take back the tap

tomorrows transcend pain
peace deserves a chance
gratitude heals my greed and grief

Tsunami of hope
peace
possibility
splendor
make our tomorrow better
and trust in our unknown God
becomes a healing balm in the Gilead
of our planetary soul

Story: Scott—A Child of the Universe

Scott is my grandnephew. He is a wonderful child, much loved and faced with many difficult physical challenges. The following reflection is dedicated to Scott and all children who embody our hope for the future.

> To be a child of the Universe—loved, wounded, incarcerated in an unresponsive body, yet in every way an inspiration.
>
> A source of self-transcendence, an opportunity to see beyond—to believe in a tomorrow not built on fantasy or buried in despair.
>
> To feel the sacredness of life present in our midst, although lacking common indicators of hope and health — something new shines through and illuminates each day.
>
> A smile, a sign of recognition, a knowing glance from the deep wells of beauty and pain shines forth from his eyes.

So we arise today and look upon the child—with love and hope. With trust we kiss his cheek and celebrate with gratitude the ground that gave him life as we celebrate our own.

A child with special needs is special to me.

Prophetic Voices

In a truly spiritual world there would be no crack; homes would be without violence; every child would have two parents; every father would have a job; the streets would be safe; and God would be fond of everyone. (Jonathan Kozol, quoting a thirteen-year-old boy)

Poetry is not a luxury. It is a vital necessity for our existence. It forms the quality of light from which we predicate our hopes and dreams toward revival and change; first into language then into idea and then into more tangible action. (André Lourde)

So encourage each other and build each other up, just as you are already doing. (Letter to the Thessalonians)

There's a dream in my soul that wants to live
A dream of oneness with all that is
A dream of a love that can heal a wounded world
Can you dream this dream with me? (Carmel Bracken)

Moment of Silence

Response: The Question of Evil

The question of evil is a great puzzle to me. An insight from Professor Patrick Flood, my freshman philosophy teacher, has remained with me to this day. It went something like this: Philosophers, theologians and others have struggled with the question of evil for many years; their response continues to be that it remains a mystery. So it is not surprising that evil remains a puzzle to me.

Classical theologians have named our struggle with evil, pain, darkness and silence, the *via negativa*. They have offered us a spiritual strategy of letting go to deal with the bitter and burdensome aspects of life. We understand that pain is an integral aspect of life. It is more than a phenomenon to be diagnosed and medicated, it is a mystery to be lived. Pain can be understood as a result of evil. However, it can also be understood as the result of our finiteness, the limits of our human condition. To some extent pain is a result of our unwillingness to embrace the limits of our lives.

Our response to pain depends on our spirituality. A healthy spirituality involves avoiding two extremes. One is denial, which may lead to substance abuse or some other destructive behavior. The other is an inordinate attachment to pain. Here we cling to pain as a substitute for pleasure. These extremes can lead to a great deal of confusion.

Meister Eckhart teaches us the spiritual practice of letting go: "When one has learned to let go and let be then one is well disposed and he or she is always in the right place within the society or in solitude."

What is your response to the circumstance and concerns that crowd your consciousness and consume your energies at this moment? How can the *via negativa* (letting go and letting be) enrich and deepen your spiritual journey? Reflect on whether that response promotes fulfillment for you, for others and for Earth.

Closing of the Day ~ The Universe Speaks of Struggle and Fulfillment

~ Our challenge is to find fulfillment in the midst of struggle, to transcend the "bitter and burdensome" aspects of existence.

~ We listen attentively to the words of Mary Oliver who writes, "I tell you this to break your heart, to break your heart open, that it never again be closed to the world."

~ We discover in our struggle "a moment of grace," a time when unprecedented change and transformation can take place.

~ We envision a seamless garment where divisions collapse and a world of enchantment emerges, a newness that heals all loss.

~ Through struggle and fulfillment we engage a crossing point of wisdom that transforms oppression, confronts dominance and gives birth to collaboration.

~ We discover fulfillment in this multi-tasking, anxious and accelerated culture.

SATURDAY

DAWN

Theme: Cultural Therapy

"He has sent me to bring goodness to the poor, to bind up hearts that are broken, to proclaim liberty to captives, freedom to those in prison." (Isaiah)

Therapy means "healing power" or "a healing quality." While we usually think of therapy as an individual pursuit, i.e., being "in therapy," the need for healing applies to our culture as well. Cultural therapy transforms utility into reverence, destruction into diversity, abuse into wonder, degradation into belonging, autism into remembering, alienation into intimacy, damage into restoration, despair into spontaneity and healing so that beauty can shine through. Through cultural therapy we can begin to understand our behavior and the behavior of others. We become agents of change in ways that restore and enhance the culture.

Reflection: Reflection: Thresholds of Compassion

Our society is in urgent need of a cultural curative. One treatment is deep cultural therapy in which we confront our personal sorrows and awaken to the realization that embedded within our broken hearts lies the pain of our world. We watch horrified as Earth is besieged and devastated by toxins – the air, earth and water poisoned, innocents choked by patriarchal oppression, peoples manipulated by terrorism and fear, individuals deprived of healthy food, intimacy and community.

Deep cultural therapy is a process that invites us to become whole again—to aspire to strategies and tactics that reinforce our radical interconnection to vitality and life. It calls us to open our heart, to fall in love again with Earth. It encourages us to grow where we live and transcend the mind-set of consumerism and nature as an object. It demands a personal response and action to transform fear into courage, anger into righteous outrage, illness into insight, complaints into compassion, competition into cooperation, woundedness into healing and emptiness into a revitalized mysticism. Deep cultural therapy is, in fact, not a strategy but a way of life.

We understand with heightened awareness that within the depth of the imagination resides our natural capacity for compassion. New science, having tied the common origin of our Universe to a beginning point in time, tells us that all life is inter-dependent and inter-connected. We learn with astonishment that humans are genetically coded to care for one another and, in fact, for every species. As our imagination awakens, we discover what it is like to experience the other. We are urged on by the prophetic voice of Sister Rosalie Bertel, "The future is wired into us."

Enduring questions remain: How did I get here? What am I called to do? Upon what support and resources can I draw in my quest? As I ponder these questions, I ask: What is the connection between the sacred truths of my tradition and the fresh insights into nature by modern science? Probing further into these questions, I realize that when I understand something new about the natural world, I simultaneously understand something new about the Divine. Within this deep and mysterious unfolding is a recognizable pattern, a hope-filled realization, that as we deepen our insights about nature, we deepen our relationship with God.

Deep cultural therapy is a profound invitation to locate our lives within the great primordial unfolding of our Universe. Together we can unite to confront the crises of our time while at the same moment envision the world as we would like it to be. It is time to bring fresh energy and new possibilities into the structures of society.

Today, we stand awake and positioned at the portal of a new and promising planetary movement. Perhaps this is the time to accept the invitation of Desmond Tutu, Nobel Peace Prize laureate, "Come, join the winning side."

Threshold Thoughts

Parting
Depart like the clouds
in the morning haze
like the river
as it rushes past the shore

To say nothing of the morning glories
in my neighbor's garden
Saint Theresa tells us
nothing lasts forever

Neither joy, nor pain
maybe even God

Settle frightened one
desperation rises like the sun
to reveal a new perception
now at peace

Rest
When all else fails
and previous accomplishments dissolve

The misguided drive
toward self-importance
takes a rest
it is then we enter
a timeless zone

A place where life and love
and plans for contribution
are set aside

Notice the cricket and crow
they proudly fulfill
their greater purpose

To fly and eat and care for the young
is all for which they hope

I want to live like that
celebrate each moment with play
work diligently each day with no good reason
love what I love and let it be
perhaps then and only then
will I discover sabbath for my soul

Story: Another Perspective

Let me finish with a story. It isn't my story. It is Kurt Vonnegut's. But I think it sums up absolutely everything the human being is called to be, whether in the past (when the story took place; you may be aware that Vonnegut was a POW in

Dresden during the saturation bombing of the city by the Americans), in the present or in the future. *In Armageddon in Retrospect,* Vonnegut writes:

> Our little prison was burned to the ground. We were to be evacuated to an outlying camp occupied by the South African prisoners. Our guards were a melancholy lot, aged Volkssturmers and disabled veterans. Most of them were Dresden residents and had friends and families somewhere in the holocaust. A corporal, who had lost an eye after two years on the Russian front, ascertained before we marched that his wife, his two children, and both of his parents had been killed. He had one cigarette. He shared it with me.

Now, that's a story! I'm not convinced a new future is necessary when there are people like this in the world.

Prophetic Voices

The next generations need a truly inspiring vision of the wonder and grandeur of life, along with the beginnings of the new technologies they will need. (Thomas Berry)

And so it was, I entered the broken world. (Heracletus)

As the trees grow, they grow hope, they grow self-confidence, they transform the land.
(Wangari Maathai)

It's a question of discipline, the little prince told me. . . . When you've finished washing and dressing each morning, you must tend your planet. (Antoine de Saint-Exupéry)

Be compassionate as your loving God is compassionate. (Gospel of John, 6:26)

This is the use of memory; for liberation. (T.S. Eliot)

Moment of Silence

Response: The Shadow

I remember a time when we gathered in Toronto and were encouraged to connect with the "shadow." When we reconvened, people were asked to celebrate and act out their shadow. The result was a room bursting with energy.

For me, the shadow is that which summons me into the hour of the unexpected. It is the unseen energy that draws me forward into what is hidden and yet to be expressed. The shadow is the dark side of my psyche, a place where molten energy is not yet formed. It is my as-yet unrealized potential, that place of ongoing exploration where adventures happen and self-discovery takes place.

Take some time as we did above to connect with the unexpressed energy that resides within your psyche. Contemplate ways to give it expression through music, poetry, dance, movement or song

DUSK

Theme: Cultural Therapy

"At an archetypal level the death-resurrection paradigm represents a shift from chaos to cosmos; cosmos characterizes the shattering of all the here and now boundaries and depicts a world of unlimited possibilities." (Leonardo Boff)

We are at the threshold of something extremely exciting, which means that we are also at the end of something. It is like watching a flying trapeze artist at work. She swings out, holding onto the bar, and then lets go with the expectation that another bar will be there to catch onto. We need to be more like her. We have to let go of the old paradigm with confidence that the new will give us something firm to hold onto.

Reflection: Our Greatest Moment

Each day we are reminded, "We live in a time of change." A five-year old girl from California captured the imagination of many. Her extraordinary ability to dribble a basketball was recorded on YouTube and broadcasted widely. Suddenly she was known. When the African-American child was asked who is her favorite person, she answered, "Barack Obama because he looks like me."

This moment together with so many others are opportunities for change and an important reminder that we stand on the shoulders of those who have gone before us. For example, today, the phrase, "Yes We Can (Si Se Puede)," has become a mantra for mobilizing and organizing current movements for change.

Looking back we realize that these words were first uttered by Delores Huerta, co-founder of the United Farm Workers (UFW) when the UFW joined the hotel workers in their "Justice for Janitors" campaign. Behind this motto, "Yes We Can," lays a full range of strategies and tactics employed by the farm workers. This cry for justice in the 21st century finds its roots in a legacy of prophets of the past. Among them is John L. Lewis who organized the United Mine Workers. Lewis was a mentor to Saul Alinsky who brought mass-based community organization to the urban areas of the United States and beyond. Fred Ross, a student of Alinsky, brought the organizing work to the farmlands of the Southwest. There, under the charismatic leadership of Cesar Chavez, they applied their organizing work to electoral politics, adopting the slogan, "Today we march, Tomorrow we vote."

Like in the past, young people today of all ages are inspired to join a cause greater than themselves. They are inspired by words similar to those uttered by Cesar Chavez, "In giving their lives, they find life. In serving others, they lose the fear that crippled them."

Jesuit priest and peace activist, John Dear, gives us a vision of a better tomorrow and challenges us to build our future on the legacy of those who have gone before. He evokes the words of Dan Berrigan who calls us to "make peace" and of Martin Luther King, Jr. who proclaimed "the choice is non-violence or non-existence." John Dear traces and celebrates our transformational history:

- The abolitionists made it possible to end slavery.
- The suffragettes made it possible for women to vote.
- The Civil Rights movement made it possible for people to be judged by the content of their character.
- The Peace movement confronted the pathology of the Vietnam War.

- The environmental movement with Rachel Carson's *Silent Spring* inaugurated the awareness that if we are to have peace on Earth, we must make peace with Earth.

Today there is fresh energy to create dynamic integration among those who are committed to social justice, ecology and spiritual fulfillment. They ask a bold question: "Is democracy compatible with free market capitalism?" These voices number themselves among the millions of leaderless and invisible groups around the world who share a common goal for a more mutually enhancing world.

Our call is to become "the new abolitionists," to build on the legacy of the past and move into a promising and unprecedented future. It is time to take the vows of risk and ambiguity, to be buoyed on by the words of Martin Luther King, Jr., "This is the greatest moment to live in all history." Then, and only then, will the child with her great basketball talent, and really all children grow up to honor the legacy of their ancestors who have made it possible.

Threshold Thoughts

Welcome Home
Miracles happen
unexpected consequences burst forth
walks along the corridor
become a passageway toward home

Hope happens
life goes on
sparrows at the window
chant their welcome

Meanwhile Darla, the cat
purrs gently on her lap
takes a contented nap
and in her feline way says
welcome home

A New Day
The day dawns like every day
sun rises, clouds part
the unexpected appears

With great uncertainty
in irreversible ways
the clock of time ticks on
open-ended futures
announce the end of things

Something new hovers at the door
opening to the threshold of tomorrow
The cosmic cycle takes another turn
while life enters yet a new place

A time to learn the lessons of the past
and dare to see a new tomorrow

Surrender acts of illusion and self-importance
to feel again the healing hand of God

Story: It's Our Time Now

The dream of inclusion for all is dangerous to those committed to the status quo and they will do what it takes to silence the voices of the dreamers. I once attended a concert given by Harry Belafonte where he shared a conversation he had

had with Nelson Mandela about setbacks in US society. Mandela's response is a wonderful statement about the meaning of working for justice: "You'll just have to keep at it until they're all one." Perhaps his advice is being realized today.

The First Congregation Church of Oakland was overflowing with an energetic and enthusiastic crowd as actor activist and civil rights leader Danny Glover stepped to the microphone. He told us a story about his five-year old grandson. It was November 4, 2008, election day in America, and the child was in tears because he could not vote for Barack Obama. His mother comforted him and said, "It's ok, I'll vote for both of us." As Danny Glover proceeded to read a poem by Langston Hughes, "Let America be America Again," the mood in the church changed. The people looked back over the past four decades and recalled the tragic deaths of Martin Luther King, Jr. and Bobby Kennedy. As the crowd reflected, they came to realize that the same vision and spirit is still here among us. With a new leader in the White House, they could now hope and dream again.

Danny Glover can tell his grandson, and through him, all children, "Yes, it's been a long walk, but it's our turn now."

Prophetic Voices

The difficulty is that the natural world is seen primarily for human use, not as made of sacred presence primarily to be communed with in wonder and beauty and intimacy…a sacred reality to be venerated. (Thomas Berry, the Great Cultural Therapist)

An increasing number of people feel the need to be in be in contact with the mystery beyond what we can see, hear, and taste, touch or think beyond the constraints of mechanistic materialism. . . .

In awe and wonder we contemplate the mystery of it all. (Albert Nolan)

It is simply opening yourself to receive the presence of God; it is like walking out of a door into the fresh air. You don't concentrate on the fresh air, you breathe it and you don't concentrate on the sunlight—you just enjoy it—it's all around. (Thomas Merton)

There arises a spirituality in which the human city is human not simply by the fact that it is made of persons and institutions; plants, the water, the pure air, the animals and healthy conditions of natural life are also to be brought together in harmony. (Leonardo Boff)

But when an insight or idea has sunk in, practice invisibly changes, the idea then opens the eye of the soul. By seeing differently, we do differently. (James Hillman)

Happy are the people who read the prophetic message, and happy are those who hear it and heed what is written in it, for the time is near. (Book of Revelations, 1:3)

This is a critical evolutionary moment…I believe that the beauty and power of the new story, the knowledge of our belonging within it, and the hope and vision the story can awaken, will bring forth the caring that bears the psychic energy needed to co-create with the Earth a viable future. (Mary Conrow Coelho)

Moment of Silence

Response: Restorative Energy

Everywhere we look today, something new is stirring. From the rubble of war, the residue of corporate greed, the demoralized halls of government and justice, there is a new urgency, a tidal wave of hope. This is not a hope predicated on economic calculations that transcend ecological destruction. Rather it is a hope arising from a deep, deep place within the human psyche that contains the restorative energy present within each soul, every blade of grass, each child of every species — an urgent impulse to live a full and abundant life. It is a hope of resurrection as we form a more intimate reconnection with Earth.

A friend of mine is fond of saying, "Who is God? God is that deep mystery that is imperceptible to the senses, yet fully present in everything that we can see, hear, feel, taste and touch." Poet William Stafford writes, "I'm listening, but I don't know if what I hear is silence or God." To paraphrase Kurt Vonnegut, "I have no need for proof of the existence of God, as I know there is beauty, wonder and belonging."

Which sense alerts you most fully to the sacred? Is what you are sensing silence or God? What stirrings inspire your journey? Is there a person (or creature or aspect of nature or something else that calls you to yourself and others) or a transitional life event that has catapulted you onto that next trapeze bar? Contemplate deeply these sacred moments and express yourself through writing of prose or poetry.

Closing of the Day ~ The Universe Speaks of Healing the Culture

~ Deep cultural therapy is enhanced by the exposure to beauty, wonder and belonging.

~ We transcend personal sorrow and awaken to the realization that deep within our broken hearts lies the pain of the world.

~ We move beyond the pathology and respond to the cry of the poor and the poor Earth.

~ This is a call to transform fear into courage, anger into moral outrage, pain into healing, emptiness into a new mysticism.

~ A call resounds to open our hearts and fall in love with Earth and her peoples, to fashion a multi-centered and inter-connected world that holds generosity, gratitude and deep interrelation.

~We each have a role to play in a world that transforms competition into cooperation, isolation into community and domination into empowerment.

~ It is a time to listen to the voice of Thomas Berry who reminds us that the God of the Cosmos is present in every blade of grass.

~ To paraphrase Kurt Vonnegut, "I have no need for proof of the existence of God as I know there is beauty, wonder and belonging"; the poet William Stafford, "I'm listening, but I don't know if what I hear is silence of God"; the prophetic proclamation of Clarissa Pinkola Estes, "You were made for these times."

AFTERWORD

Envisioning Tomorrow

"May the future be better than all the pasts." (Teilhard de Chardin)

"We would have no inner life of mind, imagination or emotion without the wonder, the beauty and the intimacy offered us by the dawn and sunset, the singing birds and the cry of the wolf, seeing the meadows and all the flowers, by the grandeur of the mountains and the vastness of the sea." (Thomas Berry)

As we envision tomorrow, we are carried forward by a collective vision of what it means to be a "cosmological person." We see that person as a lover of solitude yet deeply engaged in the defining issues of today.

This person demonstrates deep gratitude for her ancestors on whose shoulder she stands. Committed to the practice of reciprocal relationships, she is always open to change. With defining characteristics of curiosity and humor, this cosmological person finds ways to be open to "the question" and disposed to live into the answers should they emerge.

Deeply aware of the ineffable presence of divinity, this person is constantly in pursuit of "the More." Aware of the rivers of grace that stream through every molecule of existence, she seeks the empowerment and companionship of like-minded people. This cosmological person always imagines a better world for the children of all species and is prompted by the sacred impulses that nudge her forward into life.

Committed to fulfill her calling and destiny of being, she is dedicated to take up the challenges that lie ahead and to find energy and hope in the beauty, wonder and belonging that reside at the heart of the Universe. Although a challenge, she views it as a great cosmic adventure. Enveloped in mystery, she approaches the portal to unlimited possibilities as an opportunity to become engaged in the healing and transformation of Earth and her peoples.

To allow the true self to shine through is to gain the capacity to transcend the bitter, sorrowful and burdensome aspects of existence. The God of the Cosmos is present everywhere, revealed through the whirling dance of the atoms and the stars, each blade of grass, the song of every bird and, of course, the compassion given by humans to Earth, her children and ourselves.

Arc of Compassion

Wisdom flourishes and abounds
squirrel dances from limb to limb
stops to look
then darts away
blackbirds hover in the sky
surveying all of us below.

Puppies, birds, kittens
take their place in church
although already blessed
on this St. Francis day
all of life is gift, grace and promise.

Even the asphalt jungle
yes the ghetto is a chapel
where homeless saints abide
all is holy now
nothing lies outside
the compassionate embrace
of the wise and ancient one.

APPENDIX

A. PRAYER OF THE COSMOS

The Divine presence permeates all life. Each flower, child and cloud signifies the sacredness of all.

We gather as a people called forth by trust, promise and compassion. Standing on the shoulders of those who have gone before, we remember our origins and the company of the mystics and prophets who join us on this journey.

We remember and give thanks to the originating energy of the Universe, to the Ancient One of Days, whose vast generosity brought us into existence and calls us forth today.

We remember and celebrate the great and noble narrative of the Universe that reveals the depths of the past, the promise of the future, and announces with clarity and hope a profound epiphany at this incarnational moment.

We gather as a holy people called forth into circles of gratitude and proclamations of trust; we remember the scriptures of creation, those proclamations of divinity inscribed in the sacred rocks on whose foundation our planet stands.

The shimmering beauty of the trees and flowers is an exaltation of existence that shines forth in verdant wonder and rainbows of sacredness manifest everywhere in our midst.

We celebrate also our companions on the way, our cousins of creation who swim in the oceans, dance in the meadows and soar above us in the sky.

We make our eucharist today, embraced by the members of humanity who, with conscious self-awareness, illuminate our paths and show us the way.

We remember now and celebrate the family of ancestral prophets and pilgrims who have been tellers of the story, whose lives we honor and from whose inspiration we draw strength: Moses, Allah, Confucius, Buddha, Daniel, Mohammed, Isaiah, Ruth, Naomi, and others.

We honor the preexistent Word, the incarnate One, Jesus of the Cosmos and Earth who lived among us then and now permeates, illuminates and makes sacred every moment and molecule of existence.

We remember also those who have named our journey and whose voices challenge and cultivate our lives with monasteries of trust, hope and compassion.

Among those who have gone before we honor, celebrate and are inspired by Mary, Paul, Elizabeth, Peter, Mary Magdalene, Veronica, John, Luke, Matthew and Mark. We think also of the great cultural workers of yesterday and today by whose lives we are inspired and who incarnate wisdom for this sacred, defining moment.

We recall the mystics of the past and present—Meister Eckhart, Hildegard of Bingen, Teresa of Avila, John of the Cross, Julian of Norwich, Francis of Assisi, Clare, Mechtild of Magdeburg, Dante, and so many more.

We gather with deep gratitude and look back to those days long past and invite their presence and vision to inspire us and send us forth today.

Among the prophets of yesterday and today are Gandhi, Pope John XXIII, Karl Rahner, Edward Schillebeeckx, Dorothy Day, Teresa of Calcutta, Thomas Merton, Brother David Steindl-Rast, Pierre Teilhard de Chardin, Bede Griffiths, Dom Hélder Câmara, Martin Luther King Jr., Gustavo Gutiérrez, Dorothy Stang, Oscar Romero, and the many saints and martyrs anonymously inscribed in the prophetic book of life.

We include the Earth saints from the present and the past who have reminded us to honor and care for our sacred home. Numbered among those who have taught us to be open to the primary revelation of creation and whose existence has inspired literacy for life: Rachel Carson, Farley Mowat, Thomas Berry, Henry David Thoreau, John Muir, Jane Goodall, Chief Seattle, Loren Eiseley, Annie Dillard, and others.

Mindful of brokenness and beauty all around, we now recall and gather, enveloped in a world of beauty, wonder and belonging, to make our Earth an altar and to give thanks for all that was and is to be.

Conscious of the sacredness of existence — that all is holy and infused with the divine Spirit — we take these simple elements of bread and wine, offspring of Earth, sign of each, and the communion of all.

Called forth from the heart of the cosmos and planetary beauty all around, we remember the liberating journey of the Exodus, the Passover meal, the promised land, and the place that will set all the captives free.

Now, inspired by the words inscribed in our tradition and announced by Jesus of the Cosmos and the cross, we remember, signify, and say, "This is my body."

Also inspired and nourished by the blood of Earth, which irrigates our souls and activates all life, we echo and recall the words of the last supper and together we say, "This is my blood."

Together we proclaim our trust:

> I believe in the great paschal moments of the Universe, manifest in the galaxies and personified in the Cosmic Christ. I believe in the incarnational energy of the flaring forth, in the cosmic crucifixion of galaxies and stars. I believe in self-transcendence and new life embodied and expressed in the emergence of Earth, life and humans. I believe in Jesus of Nazareth and in his journey from the manger of Bethlehem, the cross of Gethsemane, the risen mystery of the empty tomb, to Transfiguration on Mount Tabor and beyond. I believe in the enveloping mystery of the Cosmic Christ, whose hidden presence manifest in every sight and sound announces beauty, wonder and belonging everywhere.

With gratitude and praise we remember and are inspired to look forward with hope and make our collective acclamation to a future that is unknown.

We remember all who have gone before and anticipate a future filled with abundant life manifest in every galaxy, species, ancestor and star. We are mindful of every species gone extinct without a resurrection, each life squandered on the battlefields of war.

From our planetary altar we behold a cosmos and a world alive with divine creative energy, pulsating, transfigured and transformed every day in every way.

Nourished for the journey, we take up our planetary task embraced by the sacred envelope of life.

Empowered by the Universe, we join our words and work with the great cosmic thrust that invites us into a future as yet unknown.

As new people, transfigured and transformed, we join the great eucharistic banquet at the dawn of a new era infused with cosmic wisdom. Grateful to the God of the Cosmos who invites us into partnership, we go forth to co-create a new world, a new heaven and a new Earth.

B. LITURGY OF THE HOURS

"As we enter the liturgy of the Cosmos, we realize that each of us has our own role to play within the entire sequence of transformations that have given shape and identity to everything that exists." (Gail Worcelo)

~Gather
~Music
~Listen

Read in silence or in community:

I believe the world provides every physical image and sensation we will ever need in order to experience the sacred, to declare the holy, if only we could learn to recognize it, if we could only hone and refine our sense of the divine, just as learn to see and distinguish with accuracy the ant on the trunk of the poplar, the Pole Star in Ursa Minor, rain coming toward us on the wind; just as we come to identify the sounds we hear, the voices of our children, the creak of the floor at the lover's footstep, the call of a finch unseen in the top of a pine, as we can detect and name the scent of cedar or sage. Might it be possible, if we try, to become so attuned to the divine that we are able to perceive and announce it with ease too? And perhaps the divine, the sacred, the holy only come into complete existence through our witness of them, our witness for them and to them ... We may be the consciousness of the universe, the way by which it can come to see and love

> and honor itself. If this is so, then our obligations are mighty and humbling. We are co-creators. We are servants. I believe we move through the sacred constantly, yet remain oblivious to its presence except during those rare, unexpected moments when we are suddenly shocked and shaken awake, compelled to perceive and acknowledge. During those brief moments we know with bone-centered conviction who it is we are; with breath-and-pulse clarity where it is we have come from; and with earth-solid certainty we know what it is we owe all our allegiance, all our heart, all our soul, all our love. (Pattiann Rogers)

All quotes below by Thomas Berry:

As the great cosmic symbolisms shine forth with new splendor we will realize that the technological attack on the natural order is not only a physical loss and degradation but that it is even more a psychic and spiritual destruction. Thus the first instinct of religious consciousness in the future must be to save … Earth as a divine voice, which, once destroyed, will no longer be heard. Without this voice it is a question whether written or spoken scriptures within our own being can be heard or understood.

As we speak of this comprehensive revelation we indicate the awakening of the vast range of human imaginative powers. A new religious, poetic, visionary power is needed. Only this can sufficiently deepen our understanding of the present, evoke the needed vision of the future or activate the vast resources of human energy needed to realize the salvific transformation … of human life for which we are destined.

We're here to hear the story and experience the dream.

The dream is at the heart of the action.

The overarching movements that gave shape and meaning to life by relating the human venture to the larger destinies of the universe.

Once we realize that the human story is inseparable from the universe story, the story that reveals the divine, the story that illuminates every aspect of our religious and spiritual life.

Our spirituality is Earth derived...the thoughts and emotions, the social forms and rituals of the human community, are as much Earth as is the soil and the rocks and the trees and the flowers.

Personal savior orientation has led to an interpersonal devotionism that quite easily dispenses with Earth except as a convenient support for life.

Christianity is developmental human time; the working out of a divine presence in the human world in terms of the Kingdom of God ... Our modern story of the universe is a new sense of the universe. These two need in some matter to be related.

This intimacy, which exists with the stars in the heavens and with the flowering forms of Earth, the presence of humans and with other members of the animal world, is unique.

The universe presents itself full of mystery and meaning ... the basic norms of human activities can be discovered from within the profoundly spiritual process that is the universe itself.

The universe is a single, vast, celebratory event. Here the poetry, the music, the mystique of the Earth all find expression ... we are able once again to hear the music and experience the depth of fulfillment that are available to us once we are attuned to the symphony around us.

The full power of ecology can only be felt in the realization that the universe, the planet Earth, and all living and non-living beings exist primarily for celebration.

We can never bring a healing to this continent until we are first blessed and first healed by this continent.

Poets are most profoundly in communion with other modes of understanding.

The terminal decade of the century is becoming a moment of grace.

We're here to learn the story and experience the dream.

Just as the ruined landscapes we see about us are the visible dreams of the past, so any future world restored in it primordial loveliness must first come into being in the dreams that arise from the primordial depths within us. Without such dreams, none of our efforts as purifying this toxic planet or establishing a viable mode of existence of the Earth will succeed.

The great story of the universe, the story of Earth, and the story of the human have seemed too distant from each other to be encompassed within a single presentation. Now, however, the urgency is such that we can no longer isolate these various components of Earth from each other. This urgency includes all the elements of the Great Story, but especially the Story of the Earth.

The greatest contribution we can make to our children is to assist them in their dreams of a world of pure air and water, sunlight and soil, where the company of living beings flourish as has not happened in recent years.

The leadership of religion that created the great civilizations of the past is now called upon to create a new type of civilization in the dawning ecological age – a civilization that will be integral with the ever-renewing transformation of the natural world.

~Silence
~Music
~Closing

PRAISES FOR *BEAUTY, WONDER AND BELONGING*

Beauty, Wonder and Belonging ...Conlon invites the reader to explore the wider horizons of human experience which he has traversed – soul-scapes both intimate and vast – aided by the revelatory maps and wise orienteers that have been his guides as he, now, becomes ours…

Kathleen Deignan, CND, PhD
Editor of*:*
Thomas Merton: A Book of Hours and
When the Trees Say Nothing: Writings on Nature, Thomas Merton

Jim Conlon writes like a pilgrim weaving a loom, threading a pathway, enveloping a membrane, leaving for the rest of us traces of a new mysticism, a more engaging spiritual wisdom for our time. Adopting the liminal images of dawn and dusk, he draws us into a more reflective engagement, centered upon the ups and downs of daily life, consistently embellished with the vision of the new cosmic story.

Diarmuid O'Murchu, MSC, Ph.D
Author of*:*
Quantum Theology, Evolutionary Faith,* and *Ancestral Grace

In this moment of history, humankind's urgent task is to live out of a unitive consciousness that honors the connectedness of all life – to become "cosmological persons." Living from such a transpersonal orientation requires that we avail ourselves to Mystery, the creative spirit who is the source of all being. In *Beauty, Wonder and Belonging* Jim Conlon invites us into the practice of "engaged cosmology," providing a space in which cosmology, tradition and person story bring us to the brink of Mystery. Written a book of hours, the reflections, poetry and quotations in *Membranes of Mystery: A Cosmic Book of Hours* invites us into a place where we begin to grow in the awareness of who we really are, cosmological beings to all that is. Allow this book to companion you, to lead you to the brink of Mystery – and then let go!

Judy Cannato, MA
Author of ***Radical Amazement*** and ***Quantum Grace***

This book is a treasure designed to accompany meditative reflections on daily life.

Rosemary Radford Ruether, PhD
Author of: ***Gaia and God, Sexism and God-Talk*** and ***Goddesses and the Divine Feminine: A Western Religious History***

Absorbed in Jim Conlon's lovely book, *Beauty, Wonder and Belonging,* beguiled by its stories and poetry, I remember as appreciatively as when I first learned it, a fine old elementary school truism, that somewhere on this endlessly turning home of ours, it is *always* dawn and it is *always* dusk – *always* midnight and *always* high noon – that at the very moment I greet this new and unformed day in prayer, my brothers and sisters half a world away are singing it to sleep.

Hour by precious hour, we do walk through *Beauty, Wonder and Belonging* – and what a wonderful thing Jim's done in urging us to slow way, *way* down and know it!

Carol Lee Flinders, PhD
Author of: ***Enduring Grace*** and ***Enduring Lives***

Jim Conlon's Book of Hours speaks to a deep hunger. It not only proclaims the sacredness of all life, it offers practices for doing that ourselves every single, ordinary day. With this book we discover that the world is our cloister

Joanna Macy
Author of *World as Lover, World as Self*

Science's discovery of the fourteen billion year evolution of the universe has to be understood as one of the most significant of human history. One of the principal spiritual challenges of the 21st century will be the creation of cultural practices enabling humans to assimilate this perplexing, new creation story. Jim Conlon's *Beauty, Wonder and Belonging* is a powerful step in this process and is wholeheartedly recommended.

Brian Swimme, PhD,
California Institute of Integral Studies
Author of:
The Universe is a Green Dragon, The Hidden Heart of the Cosmos and ***The Universe Story*** (with Thomas Berry)

Beauty, Wonder and Belonging calls us – during these critical and often disconcerting times – to remember and honor the magic, the mystery and sacredness of our unfolding evolutionary journey. It provides an important and much needed lens of hope and possibility.

Belvie Rooks, MA
Carrie Productions/producer and host of
"Conversations that Matter —
Frontiers of Race, Cosmology & Consciousness"
and contributing author of
My Soul is a Witness: African-American Women's Spirituality.

We can feel the great shifts at dawn and dusk, these two hinge moments of the day, as the veil within the sanctuary of the cosmic temple lifts, and a heightened sense of Presence is experienced within the Earth Community.

Beauty, Wonder and Belonging ask the reader to step over the threshold of these two sacred moments and join with the entire planetary community in the celebration of Being. In reading Beauty, Wonder and Belonging there is a rhythmic sense of expansion and contraction, activism and reflection and a heightened awareness that we live within these great circular gestures of Earth's dynamics.

Beauty, Wonder and Belonging is a cosmic psalter for those living and working in the monastery that is the Earth itself.

Gail Worcelo, SGM, MA
Green Mountain Monastery

Jim Conlon celebrates his week of dawns and dusks in a monastery without walls. The tone of his poetry is largely optimistic, and his optimism is eschatologically verified; "All manner of thins shall be well" as all hopeful mystics sing, looking through time into eternity. But a true mystic is also "A troubadour of hope / Trumpeting / On an ocean / Of despair." (Sunday Dusk)

Should a night of eco-catastrophe come upon us, the poetry and prayers of Jim Conlon will help us hope in a dawn of new heavens and a new earth, sure to come.

Thomas Matus, OSB, Cam, PhD
Author of ***Ashram Diary in India with Bede Griffiths***
and editor of ***Bede Griffiths: Essential Writings***

It takes a lifetime to weave a membrane of memory and mystery for these times. One must be grounded in the depth of past time and space which is present here and now. One must also carry a special generosity of heart. Both are essential if one is to painstakingly gather and weave together the threads of an unspeakably beautiful world and the words of so many human voices who call the rest of us to mend the tears in its web of right relationships.

Jim Conlon has been a weaver all his life and shares his vision and his practice for mending the loom which holds the patterns of hope for the future.

Miriam MacGillis, OP, MA
Co-founder of **Genesis Farm, Learning Center for Earth Studies**

What a delightful "prayer book" for daughters and sons, not just of the Church, but for the Universe. The most basic answer to people's question "How should I pray" is to wonder, to ponder, to experience amazement and awe. Jim Conlon offers a lovely threshold into that universe of prayer.

Father Brian Joyce, Pastor
Christ the King Church, Pleasant Hill, CA

In this book two contemplative currents coalesce: the ancient monastic one sanctifying specific hours of the day and the contemporary scientific one opening us to the wonder of cosmic consciousness. In his personalized, spiral style of presentation, Jim Conlon takes us through the realistic stages of his own journey of discovering new spiritual strength as he progressed toward integrating them. Both currents, in the gentile care of this text, are elaborated in pluriform ways: prose and poetry, anecdote and aphorism, honest revelation and reverent prayer. Too rich for any one hour or day, they invite repeated visits of each day, evoking a fresh energy for one's own participation in the Great Work. Brought together this way, they allow the reader to respond to Thomas Berry's invitation to honor the great liminal times, dawn and dusk of each day. Those who do so will have the richness of Jim Conlon's courageous journey as wise guide.

Stephen Dunn, CP, PhD
Founder of **the Elliot Allen Institute in Theology and Ecology**

What a glorious book! It reveals the splendor of a cosmic liturgy; it calls us to a new kind of praying where the regular beat of our lives is inextricably interwoven with the rhythm of the universe. Inspired by and dedicated to Thomas Berry, James Conlon's strikingly modern "Book of Hours" makes deep sense of life's mystery and silences as well as its call to awakening and greater awareness. This profoundly transformative prayer within the cosmic monastery without walls is calling us into presence and gratitude before the great mystery of being.

Ursula King, PhD
Author of ***Spirit of Fire: the Life and Vision of Teilhard de Chardin***
and ***The Search for Spirituality***

Every single morning of your life, darkness and light have been celebrating the cosmic liturgy of dawn. How often were you present to witness this wonder? Every evening, earth and sky stage the solemn light show of sunset and dusk. When was the last time you attended this ritual? Initiates enter these sacred moments in silence. For the uninitiated, James Conlon's *Beauty, Wonder and Belonging* provides words of invitation and inspiration.

Brother David Steindl-Rast, OSB, PhD
Author of: ***Gratefulness, The Heart of Prayer***
and ***Common Sense Spirituality***
www.Gratefulness.org